The Strange Laws of Old England

NIGEL CAWTHORNE

The Strange Laws of Old England

PIATKUS

PIATKUS

First published in Great Britain in 2004 by Portrait
This paperback edition published in 2007 by Piatkus Books

Reprinted 2004 (three times), 2005 (four times),
2006 (three times), 2007 (twice)

A CIP catalogue record for this book
is available from the British Library

ISBN 978-0-7499-5036-1

Design and typesetting by Paul Saunders
Printed and bound in Great Britain by
Mackays of Chatham Ltd, Chatham, Kent

Piatkus Books
An imprint of
Little, Brown Book Group
100 Victoria Embankment
London EC4Y 0DY

An Hachette Livre UK Company

www.piatkus.co.uk

Contents

Introduction

THERE ARE A GREAT MANY laws in old England – not to mention Scotland and Wales – many of which are strange. Currently there are 358 volumes of statutes at large and general public acts, occupying 22 shelves in the British Library, while there are another 682 volumes of local, personal and private acts, occupying another 50 shelves, plus a further 32 shelves of statutory instruments.

The situation was summed up in the last century by Sir Cecil Carr: 'As a collection our statute book might be summed up as beyond the average citizen's pocket to purchase, beyond his bookshelves to accommodate, beyond his leisure to study and beyond his intellect to comprehend.' And he ought to have known – Carr was the Chairman of the Statute Law Committee which began trying to tidy up the laws of old England at the end of the Second World War. Even now the job is far from over.

Yet the statutes passed by Parliament and signed by the sovereign are less than half of it. There is case law where the

judgement in each of the hundreds of thousands of cases that have passed through the judicial system can be called on as a precedent in a subsequent case and the rules of equity – fairness – that judges make up as they go along. The whole shaky edifice is found on common law, which is essentially the half-remembered customs and practices of the Anglo-Saxons' largely unwritten legal code as reinterpreted by judges sitting after the Norman Conquest.

The thing that makes English law so wonderfully strange is the absence of reason. James I – James VI of Scotland – made the mistake of looking for it. In 1607, four years after arriving from Scotland, he heard a case concerning land and gave his judgement, only to have it overturned on the grounds that the case belonged to the common law. He said that he thought the law was founded on reason, and that he and others had reason, as well as the judges, but England's Lord Chief Justice, Sir Edward Coke soon set him straight. He said that it was true that:

> God had endowed His Majesty with excellent science, and great endowments of nature; but His Majesty was not learned in the laws of his realm of England, and causes which concern the life, or inheritance, or goods, or fortunes of his subjects are not to be decided by natural reason but by the artificial reason and judgement of the law, which law is an act which requires long study and experience before that a man can attain the recognisance of it.

When James took this amiss and claimed that challenging his authority was treason the Lord Chief Justice replied that, in England, although the King was set above men, he was set under God and the law. James should have known better – eight years before, he had been rebuffed in Scotland by the Court of Sessions which, in his presence, refused to decide a case as he had instructed.

Coke continued to assert the supremacy of the common law over the King's authority and was dismissed in 1616 but returned to public life after violently abducting his 14-year-old daughter and marrying her, much against her will, to Sir John Villiers, brother of the influential Duke of Buckingham. After a short jail term, Coke came up with the Petition of Right against Charles I, and insisted on the right of a subject to sue the King. That right was only abolished in 1947.

Magna Carta

But surely the basis of English law is Magna Carta, the foundation of liberty in Britain, Ireland, America and the Commonwealth – or so we are told. In fact, of the 60 clauses of the Great Charter signed by King John at Runnymede in June 1215, only three are still in force. Revision started very early on and the charter was reissued in 1216 under John's son, Henry III (1216–1272), omitting things that pertained to the political situation in 1215. For example, the original document referred to a disagreement between the King and his barons. Henry III was just nine years old at the time and the council of regency which ruled the country for him was made up of the very barons who had forced John to sign the document and now clearly wanted to expunge any mention of unpleasantness.

Magna Carta was revised again in 1217, this time omitting clauses relating to forests, which were transferred into a separate forestry charter. Then, in 1225, with Henry's coming of age, it was reissued once again, with another new version in 1264, after Henry had experienced his own problems with the barons.

When Henry died in 1272, he was succeeded by his son Edward I, aka Edward Longshanks, who sought to codify the law. He 'inspected' Magna Carta and included it on his new statute rolls in 1297, by which time it was down to just 37 clauses. These, the document said, were 'to be kept in our Kingdom of England forever'. Since then a further 34 clauses have been repealed.

As it was, Edward I's version remained intact for over five centuries until George IV opened the floodgates by repealing

Clause 26 concerning inquests under the Offences Against the Person Act of 1828 and 1829. A further 15 clauses were repealed by the Statute Law Revision Act of 1863 and the Statute Law (Ireland) Revision Act of 1872. By the end of her reign Queen Victoria was responsible for the demise of yet another six clauses, and the lawmakers were chipping away at Magna Carta right up to 1969, when six more clauses were removed – including the one that guarantees townsmen and freemen the right to build bridges wherever they liked, as in Henry III's time.

So all that remains are just three:

(1) First, We have granted to God, and by this our present Charter have confirmed, for Us and our Heirs for ever, that the Church of England shall be free, and shall have all her whole Rights and Liberties inviolable. We have granted also, and given to all the Freemen of our Realm, for Us and our Heirs for ever, these liberties under-written, to have and to hold to them and their Heirs, of Us and our Heirs for ever.

(9) The City of London shall have all the old Liberties and Customs. Moreover We will and grant, that all other Cities, Boroughs, Towns, and the Barons of the Five Ports, and all other Ports, shall have all their Liberties and free Customs.

(29) No Freeman shall be taken or imprisoned, or be disseised [deprived] of his Freehold, or Liberties, or free Customs, or be outlawed, or exiled, or any otherwise destroyed; nor will We not pass upon him, nor condemn him, but by lawful judgement of his Peers, or by the Law of the Land. We will sell to no man, we will not deny or defer to any man either Justice or Right.

Along with Magna Carta, it is interesting to note that Henry III also signed a law decreeing the death penalty for anyone found killing, wounding or maiming fairies.

Habeas Corpus

There is no mention of habeas corpus – the cornerstone of liberty – in Magna Carta, which did not appear until 464 years later with the Habeas Corpus Act of 1679. This came about because a lady liked a drink or two. One night in 1621, Alice Robinson and her husband were holding a rowdy, drunken party at their home in High Holborn, London. A passing constable heard 'a brawling, fighting noise' and entered the house to investigate. Inside, he alleged, he found 'men and women in disordered and uncivil accompanying together', so the party-pooping policeman accused Alice of keeping the whole parish awake with her revelry. When she swore at him, he arrested her and she was imprisoned in the Clerkenwell House of Correction.

Apparently Alice's fellow revellers missed her wild parties and pushed for her release, eventually forcing the authorities to bring her before the courts. At the Old Bailey she told a harrowing tale, alleging that she had been stripped and given 50 lashes at the Clerkenwell House of Correction.

'I swooned,' she said, 'my flesh being torn by the whips.'

She had been forced to sleep on the bare earth and fed nothing but water and black bread, which was harsh even by the standards of the time. When it transpired that she was pregnant, there was an outcry, the jury acquitted her and the constable who had taken her into custody found himself in

Newgate Prison on the grounds that he had arrested her without a warrant – and the justice of the peace who had signed the warrant for her detention was reprimanded.

The result was the Habeas Corpus Act which takes it name from the first words of the writ issued to enforce it: '*Habeas corpus ad subjiciendum*', which means 'You should have the body for submitting'. Once the writ had been presented a gaoler had to produce the prisoner, or their corpse, within three days. This means that the authorities cannot hold a person for an unreasonable amount of time before releasing them or bringing them before a court, and is the rock that individual liberty is built on throughout the common-law countries.

However, it took some time after Alice's release for the Habeas Corpus Act to reach the statute books as the Civil War was taking place at the time. In fact, the Act may not be a law at all because it was not actually approved by both Houses of Parliament. After the Restoration, the Habeas Corpus bill had

to be introduced several times, each time being passed swiftly by the Commons before meeting stiff opposition in the House of Lords. Eventually it was passed by a disgraceful piece of chicanery. According to the Bishop of Salisbury, Gilbert Burnet, on the third reading:

> Lords Grey and Norris were named to be tellers. Lord Norris, being a man subject to the vapours, was not at all times attentive to what he was doing. So a very fat lord coming in, Lord Grey counted him for ten, as a jest a first; but seeing Lord Norris had not observed it, he went on with his misreckoning of ten; so was it reported to House, and declared that they who were for the bill were the majority, though it indeed went on the other side.

Certainly some deceit was involved – the vote in the House of Lords was recorded as 57 to 55, even though the minute book of the Lords says that there were only 107 peers present. Realising that something was amiss, Lord Chancellor Shaftesbury, a fervent supporter of the bill, got to his feet and spoke for nearly an hour on several other matters, during which time a number of peers entered and left the House, so it was impossible to have a recount. As Parliament was reaching the end of its session, the bill received royal assent without any further ado.

CHAPTER ONE

Curious Courts

HE STRANGE LAWS OF OLD England are enforced by a number of curious courts, some of which still sit today while others are simply in abeyance because no one has taken the trouble to abolish them.

The Court of Chivalry

England's Court of Chivalry ceased to be used in the eighteenth century, but after a recess of 219 years it sat again in 1954 to decide a case between Manchester Corporation and the city's Palace of Varieties. The Corporation claimed that the theatre was illegally displaying the city's coat of arms on its curtain, which the theatre admitted.

In fact, it had displayed the city's coat of arms on its curtain for over 20 years and in its official seal for over 60 years without complaint. Its defence was that the Court of Chivalry had no jurisdiction in the case as the statutes governing the Court, signed by Richard II in 1384 and 1389, only gave it authority to judge questions involving feats of arms. Indeed, the proceedings of the Court of Chivalry are the forerunner of all courts martial.

The plaintiffs argued that the Court of Chivalry had judged such matters since then, that using a court of arms without permission was 'libel' and that the Court of Chivalry was the only court with the authority to adjudicate as, in matters concerning coats of arms, the civil courts had no authority – except in the case of Kingston-upon-Hull, whose arms had been granted by a private Act of Parliament in 1952.

Counsel for the Palace of Varieties conceded that the Court had indeed made judgements in the matter of coats of arms previously, but argued that the Court was not properly constituted without a Lord High Constable. This was an hereditary post and it had been vacant since the last holder was executed in the Tower of London by order of Cardinal Wolsey in 1521. Although a surrogate is appointed at each coronation, all judgements made by the Court since 1521, the defence argued, were illegal.

For this historic hearing, the Court sat in the College of Arms in London with the full panoply of heralds in tabards and officers in full-bottomed wigs. By a curious quirk, it operated under the old Roman law, not the common law of England, but the statutes governing it were written in Norman French, which caused considerable problems for all involved. However, Lord Goddard, sitting as surrogate for the Earl Marshal, the Duke of Norfolk, decided with impeccable logic that the Court was not sitting for the first time since 1735 simply to find it had no jurisdiction, or that its judgements were invalid, found for the plaintiffs and ordered the Manchester Palace of Varieties to pay £300 costs.

Although money changed hands, the case was actually brought to re-establish the Court, since when it has imposed heavy fines on anyone, for example, creating mock coats of arm, and has taken upon itself the right to decide who orders and directs the funerals of all those who carry arms registered with the College of Arms.

Lyon rampant

Things are even more complicated in Scotland. In 1978, Denis Pamphilon, managing director of his family's linen merchants in St Albans, Hertfordshire, was threatened with the death penalty by the Lyon Court – Scotland's Court of Chivalry – for making souvenir bedspreads to celebrate the Scottish football team's appearance in the World Cup. Like most people, Mr Pamphilon believed that the death penalty had been abolished in the United Kingdom in 1965, but in fact, the Murder (Abolition of Death Penalty) Act of 1965 had left some loopholes. Capital punishment still applied in the cases of treason and piracy on the high seas and, until the Criminal and Disorder Act of 1998, offenders could still be hanged for committing arson in a naval dockyard. Mr Pamphilon had been charged under a law of 1592, which had never been repealed, and the death penalty stood.

The offending bedspread had on it a magnificent red lion rampant, a prominent symbol of Scotland and her football team. All would have been well had he confined his activities to south of the border, where England supporters we still sulking, having failed even to qualify. But being a canny businessman he spotted the real market for his firm's product was the other side of the Tweed, so he advertised it in the Scottish newspapers – which brought down upon him the wrath of the Scottish authorities. Hauled before the Lyon Court, he was charged with 'usurpation'. The lion rampant was part of the Queen's Scottish Arms and the use of it by other people was prohibited by the Act of 1592, the punishment for which was decapitation. Fortunately, the procurator fiscal to the Lyon Court did not demand the maximum penalty – instead of losing his head, Mr Pamphilon was fined £100 a day for as long as the usurpation continued.

A penitent and rather relieved Mr Pamphilon said that he would no longer be advertising the bedspreads in Scotland, by which time Scotland had been knocked out of the World Cup. Indeed other companies who had linked their products to the success of the Scottish team had withdrawn their advertising after the first round months before, following Scotland's humiliating draw with Iran, which was in the midst of an Islamic revolution. The World Cup was over and the Scottish fans wanted to forget all about it.

Flushed with this success, the Lyon Court proceeded to warn both the Scottish National Party and Glasgow Rangers for using the saltire – or St Andrew's Cross – with a lion rampant as their emblems. Inverclyde District Council had previously been banned from using the emblem on their flag after the region had been created in the 1975 reorganisation of local government.

The Prize Court

While the Court of Chivalry had jurisdiction over arms deployed on land, the Admiralty Court maintained the rule of law at sea. According to the Admiralty, this jurisdiction was established in the reign of Edward I (1239–1307), but the first records of the Court sitting occur about 1360 during the reign of Edward III.

Originally there were three courts, one for each of the three admirals who had authority over different parts of the coastline. But a single High Court of the Admiralty was formed in the fifteenth century, with jurisdiction over all crimes involving English ships and crews that were committed at sea. The Court used the same procedures as common-law courts, but in matters concerning trade and shipping, which were by necessity more international in nature, it used Roman civil law.

In the nineteenth century, the criminal element of their work was transferred to the common-law courts, leaving the

Admiralty Court with jurisdiction over cases involving collisions, salvage and cargo. Eventually the Admiralty Court was merged with the High Court of Justice.

In its heyday one of the Admiralty Court's main tasks was to crack down on piracy. However, it set up a separate Prize Court which re-registered captured ships as British. This occurred at an astonishing rate, especially at the height of British sea power during the Napoleonic Wars. Between 1792 and 1812, 48,607 foreign ships – over six millions tons of shipping – became British, in one year alone, the Court re-registering over 4,000 ships. The Admiralty Court still maintains jurisdiction over prizes, with appeal to the Judicial Committee of the Privy Council, although the Prize Court now only sits in times of war.

The court that never sits

Another court that makes rulings on matters of heraldic distinction is the Earl Marshal's Court, although it came under attack by the young MP, Edward Hyde – later the Lord Chancellor, Lord Clarendon – who denounced it as a 'tool of oppression' in his maiden speech in 1640.

He cited a number of outrageous cases. In one of these a man had been ruined by a huge fine imposed by the Court, his crime being that, in an argument with a boatman who had tried to overcharge him, he had called the swan on the waterman's badge a 'goose'. The Court decided that, as the swan on the waterman's badge was the crest of an earl, the defendant had insulted the upper classes and punished him severely for 'dishonouring' the crest.

[14]

In another, a tailor had politely asked a customer of 'gentle blood' – that is, he had a pedigree registered with the College of Heralds – if he would mind paying his bill. The man, outraged by this insolence, threatened the tailor with violence, whereupon the tailor then had the temerity to observe that 'he was as good a man as his creditor'. This was taken to be an attack on the aristocracy and the tailor was hauled in front of the Earl Marshal's Court where he was dismissed with a reprimand – provided he tear up the bill.

Edward Hyde pointed out that, in just two days, the Earl Marshal, sitting alone, had awarded more damages than had been awarded by juries in all the actions that had been tried in all the courts in Westminster in a whole judicial term. Furthermore, Hyde maintained that the Earl Marshal's Court was a 'mere usurpation' that had only sprung up during the reign of Charles I and had first sat in 1633. The House of Commons agreed that, left unchecked, the Court's powers could be established in law by constant usage. Although they never passed a bill to abolish it, the Earl Marshal was shamed by the criticism and 'his court never presumed to sit afterwards'.

Courts leet

There is a whole tier of the feudal justice system that has miraculously survived since Norman times, called the courts leet. The word 'leet' is Anglo-French and is related to the old word 'litte' which is still in use in Scotland, meaning a list of candidates selected for an office.

In Norman times, justice was administered at the level of the manor. Under the national, royal or Crown courts, there were courts baron, where the lord of the manor settled disputes and generally administered his estates. They were normally held every three weeks but had no right to deal with crimes or punish offenders, this being left to the court leets, which met usually every six months under the presidency of the lord of the manor's steward, who sat with a jury. Most towns and villages in the country had a court leet and, unlike now, the jury was selected from among the people who knew the prisoner, and also knew the background to the case. The courts leet also provided local government, policing trading standards and employing local officials.

Although there is fragmentary evidence of the workings of manorial courts in Anglo-Saxon times, custumals and surveys survive in a written form from around 1180 to 1240. The earliest surviving court roll is for the manor of Bec Abbey and dates from 1246. In the 1270s and 1280s, lords of the manor began keeping manorial court records, following the example of the King's courts.

The courts also upheld the 'frankpledge' system, which can be traced back to the time of King Canute (1016–1035). At that time, every man had to be part of a hundred – an administrative group of a hundred households – which put up a surety for his good behaviour. A freeholder's land was sufficient pledge, but the tenants of a manor had to be bound by a frankpledge of twelve, or a tithe of ten, with each tenant in the group responsible for the conduct of the others. They were also responsible to raise a 'hue and cry' to catch fleeing offenders. The frankpledge involved another system of courts known as the View of Frankpledge. Freemen – that is, freeholders – also attended in some manors. However, by the late Middle Ages the two systems had merged and court rolls were often headed 'The Court Leet with View of Frankpledge'.

By that time, serious cases were judged by circuit courts with courts leet sitting only on petty misdemeanours, this function being gradually taken over by justices of the peace sitting in magistrates courts causing manorial courts to go into terminal decline, many disappearing altogether. For example, courts leet once sat in the Southwark area of London, but lost their jurisdiction when the City of London bought the manors on the south bank of the Thames from Edward VI in 1550 for £642 2s 1d.

In the seventeenth century, the remaining courts leet lost the power to imprison and after the 1880s courts leet no longer imposed fines. The Law of Property Act of 1925 abolished more of the old manorial rights. Then in 1977 the Administration of Justice Act aimed to do away with all court barons and courts leet completely, although a few survived and some 30 or so manorial courts still sit in England today, the most well known being the Court of Verderers which regulates the New Forest.

Stannary courts

Even older than the courts leet are the stannary courts, which are a legacy from the legal system of the Cornish Celts, predating the arrival of the English. The stannary system takes its name from *stannum* – the Latin for tin – and was made up of a series of grand juries that controlled the activities of mining companies and protected the Cornish tinners and their families. It also established the right of all Cornish tinners to stake individual claims to dig for tin or other minerals, and for centuries the English Parliament recognised the 'lawful right, profit, privilege or easement to which the tinners of Cornwall are claimed to be entitled'.

After the Norman Conquest the ancient customs and privileges of the 'Stannaries of Cornwall' were recognised by a charter in 1150, and in 1198 a letter from the warden of the stannaries spelled out the rights of the mines and miners. In 1201, King John granted a new charter to the Cornish stannaries confirming the tinners' rights to dig for tin and turf for smelting it, and allowing them to work 'at all times freely and peaceably and without hindrance from any man, everywhere in moors and in the fees of bishops, abbots and counts, and of buying faggots to smelt the tin without waste of forest, and diverting streams for their works, as by ancient usage they have been wont to do'. The only magistrate to have jurisdiction over the tinners was to be their warden, who alone was allowed to summon them from their work to answer either civil or criminal charges.

Magna Carta makes mention of them, one clause saying that 'no lord should lose the services of his men whether they dug tin or not'. By that time the stannaries had come under the rule of the Earls of Cornwall. After the death of King John, his son Henry III reconfirmed the charter to the Cornish tinners and the stannaries became a state within a state, continuing to have their own laws and their own system of taxation.

The independence of the stannaries was diminished somewhat in 1337 when Edward the Black Prince, son of King Edward III, became the first Duke of Cornwall. The Plantagenets controlled the stannaries until the dynasty fell with the death of Richard III, but in 1485 the new Tudor king Henry

VII gave them back their ancient privileges by granting the power of veto of any statute concerning tin, to 1,500 Cornish tinners. These men and their families represented over half the population of Cornwall. Under the Charter of Pardon of 1508, the tinners' veto was to be exercised through 24 representatives, six from each stannary, and, through letters patent, the Westminster Parliament affirmed 'that no Statutes etc., by us our heirs and Successors shall be made unless by Assent and Consent of the aforesaid twenty-four Stannators'.

Elizabeth I reconfirmed the Charter of 1508 and issued her own letters patent. As there was no Duke of Cornwall at that time, Sir Walter Raleigh was appointed Lord Warden of the Stannaries and Lieutenant General of Cornwall.

In 1650, under the Commonwealth, Cromwell abolished the stannary regulations, but Charles I re-established the rights of the stannary courts, their legal authority being confirmed yet again by the Bill of Rights in 1688. Then in 1752, the stannary parliament was convened by writ of the then Duke of Cornwall – comprising 24 stannators and 24 assistants, each elected by the tinners – and asserted its power to veto English legislation, which it considered detrimental to Cornish interests, a direct challenge to the authority of the English state. In 1829, there was a report on the laws and jurisdiction of the stannaries of Cornwall and in 1836 the Stannaries Courts Act extended the common law over the tin mines. The last stannary court sat in 1896, although some Cornish nationalists still claim the jurisdiction of the stannary law as it has been enshrined in English law for so long, and was established by long practice and tradition. The last of the Cornish tin mines were closed down in the 1980s.

Ecclesiastical courts

The Clergy Act of 1485 gave 'archbishops and bishops, and other ordinaries [clergymen] having episcopal jurisdiction' the authority to 'punish and chastise such priests, clerks and religious men' convicted of

> advoutry [adultery], fornication, incest or any other fleshly incontinency by committing them to ward and prison, there to abide for such time as shall be thought to their discretions convenient for the quality and quantity of their trespass … and that none of the said archbishops, bishops or other ordinaries aforesaid be thereof chargeable of, to, or upon any action of false or wrongful imprisonment, but that they be utterly thereof discharged in any of the cases aforesaid by virtue of this Act.

However their sanctions were limited. They could impose a penance, defrock a priest or, at the very worse, inflict excommunication.

Benefit of clergy

Anyone who could claim that they had been ordained could take 'benefit of clergy' and be handed over to the ecclesiastical courts, a useful device for avoiding the death penalty. As almost everyone could claim some relationship with the Church, simply being literate could get you off, the usual test being to read a verse from Psalm 51, which became known as the 'neck verse' as it could save your neck. The system was so widely abused that a rule came in that you could claim benefit of clergy only once. Indeed, from the sixteenth century, a number of statutes were passed, specifying that the punishment should be death 'without benefit of clergy'. Later those opting to claim benefit of clergy were pardoned on the condition that they agreed to be transported to the American colonies. As the practice of transportation grew during the eighteenth century, with or without the benefit of clergy, this loophole was eventually abolished early in the nineteenth century.

Not in the churchyard

The ecclesiastical courts were banned by Cromwell during the Commonwealth, but their power was restored in 1661, and they are still technically responsible for the prosecution of cases of adultery and fornication to this day, although the common-law courts have largely taken over their role and the government has gradually curtailed their power. For example, in 1787, George III signed the Ecclesiastical Suits Act which said:

No suit shall be commenced in any ecclesiastical court for fornication, or incontinence, or for striking or brawling in church or churchyard, after the expiration of eight calendar months from the time when such offence shall have been committed; nor shall any prosecution be commenced or carried out for fornication at any time after the parties shall have lawfully intermarried.

CHAPTER TWO

Fabulously Feudal

NTIL HENRY III BEGAN to record and reorganise the laws of the land, the law was pretty much what those in power said it was. Under Saxon feudalism, lords ruled over the peasants with a rod of iron – for the slightest offence, a master or mistress might order a servant to be tortured or even beaten to death. For breaking a dish or spilling wine, a servant might have his or her ears cut off, nose slit or lose a hand, according to the whim of the lord or lady. While murderers and thieves could find sanctuary in a church, this privilege was not extended to servants, who could be dragged forcibly from the altar.

Saxon law

The Saxon legal system comprised a series of courts and a Witenagemot – a central council that advised the King on new laws and the distribution of land. Criminals convicted of misdemeanours – that is, crimes not subject to the death penalty – were scalped, branded or had their noses slit or their eyes put out. King Aethelstan (d. 939) even decreed that a counterfeiter would lose one hand before going to the gallows.

Flogging was commonplace – it is said that the mother of King Ethelred (978–1016) beat him so severely as a child that, for the rest of his life, he could not bear the sight of a whip; under his rule public punishments were mild and he seldom passed death sentences. However, in Saxon times, a man could beat his wife without incurring a penalty and whipping slaves was thought of as no worse than whipping animals. A slave had no real value and would be mutilated or killed at his owner's pleasure, which is why there were stocks and whipping posts outside every castle.

Nevertheless the Saxon system was not altogether barbarous. The enlightened Alfred the Great (871–899) introduced strict rules of fines and criminal compensation. Victims received 6 shillings for a mutilated ear, 9 shillings for a stab to the nose, 20 shillings for the loss of a thumb and 50 shillings for the loss of an eye. Killing a nobleman cost 150 cows or 250 gold pieces; killing a freeman cost 100 cows or 200 gold pieces; killing a serf cost just a single cow. Naturally, these fines applied only to the upper classes.

Ethelred's successor Canute, a Dane, was the first King of England to introduce something like a code of law, including the law of 'Englishry'. After he invaded in 1014 he sent most of his troops back to Denmark so that 'the rest should be safe in life and limb … any Englishman who killed any of them should suffer punishment. If the murderer could not be discovered, the township or hundred was fined.'

∽

The Normans

William the Conqueror (1066–1087) preserved the Saxon legal system, including the courts of the shires and hundreds, as a way to control his barons, and an excellent means of collecting taxes.

William also maintained Canute's law of 'Englishry'. When the body of a murder victim was found, if it could not be proved that he was an Englishman, it was assumed that he was French and the local town was fined. He also extended the frankpledge so that 'every landless man shall have a lord who shall answer for his appearance in the courts of law'.

Another innovation was the introduction to England of 'Forest Law', which was widespread on the Continent, and granted his feudal lords hunting rights and the sole rights to cut down trees on the lands that he gave them. William himself was inordinately fond of hunting and cleared vast areas, moving large numbers of villagers and peasants to make way for the chase.

The *Anglo-Saxon Chronicle* says: 'whosoever slew a hart, or a hind should be deprived of his eyesight. As he forbade men to kill the harts, so also the boars; and he loved the tall deer as if he were their father. Likewise he declared respecting the hares that they should go free. His rich bemoaned it, and the poor men shuddered at it.'

One of the areas he cleared was the New Forest in Hampshire. Like other deer parks, it was policed by William's foresters who were employed to protect the game, and anyone caught poaching was liable to lose their testicles as well as their eyes.

The situation deteriorated under his son William Rufus (1087–1100) and Henry I (1100–1135) who, it was said, had 'an army of evil men' to enforce the Forest Laws. Indeed, when Henry II (1154–1189) became king, it was 'the custom for the royal foresters to be a complete law unto themselves, they put to death and mutilated whom they would without any trial whatever, or with but the mockery of the water-ordeal, a farce which had already been condemned by the Church, but which was very fashionable with ruffians who were anxious to secure a conviction'.

Matters came to a head when some foresters seized a priest with the intention of extorting money from him, but when the Bishop of Lincoln threatened them with excommunication they let him go. Although the Forest Laws were administered from then on with something approaching justice, the feudal lord still had absolute power over his family. Robert de Belesme, Earl of Shropshire, Arundel and Shrewsbury, one of the most powerful and defiant barons of Norman times, tore the eyes out of his own children when they hid their faces behind his cloak in a game, and had his wife locked in fetters and thrown into a dungeon, only to have his servants drag her to his bed each night before returning her to the dungeon in the morning, which can hardly have promoted marital harmony. Not that that would have mattered to Robert de Belesme – he refused to ransom his captives, preferring to have both men and women impaled on stakes. Needless to say, even his friends were wary of him – he could be chatting away one minute then suddenly plunge his sword into the other person's side and roar with laughter.

The Plantagenets

The Plantagenets were little better. On his way to the Third Crusade, Richard the Lionheart (1189–1199) made a law against thieving sailors, which said: 'Whosoever is convicted of theft shall have his head shaved, melted pitch poured upon it, and the feathers from a pillow be shaken over it, that he may be known; and shall be put on shore on the first land which the ship touches.'

Meanwhile the domestic situation was improving when the building of prisons was begun following the Assize of Clarendon in 1166. In the prisons, all privately run, inmates had to pay for their upkeep and gaolers were particularly harsh on those who failed to do so. In 1290, the gaoler at Newgate bound a prisoner so tightly with irons that his neck and spine were broken, while in 1384, at Sarum gaol, the gaoler kept a prisoner in the stocks so long one winter that his feet rotted away.

Property laws

Nowadays, property is held either freehold or leasehold, but there used to be a third way – copyhold. The lord of the manor would rent out part of his land, giving the tenant a copy of the manorial court roll, listing the names of the tenants. The tenant held the tenancy at the will of the lord of the manor and 'according to the custom of the manor', which meant he was subject to the laws laid down by the lord of the manor, but was judged in a 'customary court' rather than in the court baron like a freeholder.

Copyhold lands were usually held only for the lifetime of the tenant and could not be handed on to his heirs, however some lords of the manor allowed heirs to inherit on the payment of a fine. To pass the tenancy to a third person, the tenant would have to surrender it – usually by handing over a rod, some straw or a glove – to the lord of the manor who, on payment of a fine, would transfer the copyhold to the new tenant and enter his name on the manorial court roll. The system, also called villeinage, ended in the reign of Edward IV (1461–1483), when judges stopped lords of the manor evicting copyholders without just cause.

In England all land ultimately belongs to the sovereign – even those granted tracts of land by William the Conqueror had to pay rent, in either cash or military service. A knight who held an area of 'twelve ploughlands' – worth £20 during the time of Edward I (1272–1307) and Edward II (1307–1327) – had to attend his lord at wars for 40 days a year, if called upon. If he had only half that area, he would only have to attend for 20 days, and so on, in proportion.

Of course, not every knight wanted to ride off to battle whenever the King demanded it. By the reign of Henry II, they were let off attending wars in person if they paid up and soon a scutage – a tax in lieu of military service – was levied on all tenants in the land. Then, in Magna Carta, King John agreed that no scutage could be imposed without Act of Parliament.

Tenure of land also gave a knight certain rights over his off-spring and wards. He could marry them off for money but if they refused a suitable match, they would have to pay him a sum equal to the amount he would have made from the marriage. And if they married without his consent, they would forfeit double their market value. But by the reign of Charles II (1660–1685) all knightly duties and privileges – even the right to profit from the marriage of children – were done away with.

Serjeanty

Another form of ancient tenure was grand serjeanty. Instead of having to go and fight in wars, the recipient held land in return for carrying the King's banner, or his sword – or being his but-ler, or champion, or some officer at his coronation.

Tenure by cornage was another type of grand serjeanty. Land rights were granted by the King in return for blowing a horn when the Scots or some other enemy invaded.

Sometimes the conditions of tenure were not altogether serious. Brienston in Dorset was held in grand serjeanty on the grounds that the tenant should supply a man to go before the King's army when he made war in Scotland – some records say Wales – for 40 days bareheaded and barefoot, in his shirt and linen drawers, holding a bow in one hand and an arrow without feathers in the other.

In petit serjeanty, land was granted for sending the King an instrument of war – a bow, a sword, a lance, an arrow – every year. The grants made to the Duke of Marlborough and the Duke of Wellington for their military service to the country are of this type. To this day, the Duke of Marlborough sends the Blenheim Standard to the sovereign at Windsor on 13 August every year – the anniversary of the Battle of Blenheim – as rent for Blenheim Palace, while the current Duke of Wellington is obliged to present the Queen with a small tri-colour every year at the Waterloo Dinner, held on 18 June – Waterloo Day – as rent for the estate at Stratfield Saye, which a grateful nation gave the first Duke in 1817.

In return for the tenure of Bury House, Sir Charles Mill had to give George III a brace of milk-white greyhounds each time the King entered the New Forest, and he always kept a litter in readiness. The Dukes of Athol hold their estate at Blair Athol on the condition that they present a white rose to the sovereign every time he or she visits.

Feudal conveyancing

In Saxon times, conveyancing was done by handing over a twig or some turf – in Scotland 'earth and stone' was the means used to transfer the ownership of property – which must have worked out considerably cheaper than today's arrangements.

In fact, feudal methods of conveyancing continued until surprisingly recently. Before the 1844 Transfer of Property Act introduced modern conveyancing, the ownership of a house in England was transferred from one person to another by handing over the ring or fastening from the front door, which was known in Scotland as transfer by 'hasp and staple'.

Ecclesiastical offices were handed over with a priest's cap, or biretta, and Scotland itself was given to England in 1175 when King William the Lion handed over his cap, lance and saddle to the King of England at a ceremony in St Peter's, York, admittedly under duress, having been taken prisoner by the English the year before. England itself was given away by Richard the Lionheart when he handed over his bonnet to the Holy Roman Emperor after being captured in Austria in 1192.

Trial by fire

Trial by ordeal was common in medieval times. The accused would be forced to carry a red-hot piece of metal a set distance – usually the length of the nave of a church – or walk blindfold over a bed of coal. If they emerged unscathed, or the wounds healed quickly, they would be found not guilty.

When Queen Emma, the mother of Edward the Confessor (1042–1066), was accused of a 'criminal intrigue' with Alwyn, Bishop of Winchester, she was forced to walk blindfold over nine red-hot ploughshares – one for each of the manors she was accused of giving to her lover. Not only did she manage this, but also when she had done it she innocently asked when the ordeal was going to begin. This restored her reputation and convinced the populace of her innocence to such a degree that she gave another 21 manors to the Bishop without eliciting a murmur. Trial by ordeal was banned by the Pope in 1215, though it took some time before the ban was implemented in England.

Trial by combat

Until 1818, it was still possible to claim trial by battle in England. Since the days of jousting and knights errant, in the absence of direct evidence, all civil, criminal and military cases could be settled theoretically by 'judicial combat' of a 'wager of battle'. The accused had the right to challenge his accuser to settle the dispute by force of arms. As in the opening scene of Shakespeare's *Richard II*, the fight took place in front of the Court, and God was expected to give victory to the innocent or injured party. It was often used to answer charges of treason.

There were strict rules. In civil and military cases, the disputing parties could nominate deputies, but the principals would be held responsible for the outcome. In criminal trials no deputies were allowed. The accused had to see the action through in person unless they were a woman, an infant, a man over sixty, blind or lame. No commoner was allowed to challenge a peer of the realm and, for some obscure reason, citizens of London were exempt.

Before the contest, each combatant had to attest his willingness to fight with the words: 'For what I speak, my body shall make good on this earth, or my divine soul answer it in heaven.'

The rules also specified that you could not employ sorcery or witchcraft, and the battle was to continue until dusk fell and the stars appeared. If the accused was killed, his blood was attainted, robbing his heirs of his lands and titles. If, instead, he was forced to submit, he was condemned to the more lenient, though ignominious, punishment of hanging, with no attainder, provided he accepted his fate without protest. The defeated party was also allowed to life on in disgrace as a recreant, provided he retracted everything unreservedly and swore that anything he had said was false.

The wager of battle was last invoked in 1817 after Abraham Thornton was accused of murdering a woman called Mary Ashford, of Erdington, near Birmingham, who had been killed on her way back from a dance one morning. Thornton, her partner of the previous night, was arrested, tried and acquitted, but the dead woman's brother, William Asford, was not satisfied. He gathered fresh evidence and when he appealed against the verdict a new trial was ordered, but Thornton's counsel argued that no man could be tried twice for murder, except by wager of battle in front of the King. When his claim was upheld by the courts Thornton then challenged Ashford to combat, but Ashford refused on the grounds that he was no match for Thornton physically, and so Thornton was freed. The following year, trial by battle was abolished by statute as being 'a mode of trial unfit to be used'.

Trial by swallowing

In Anglo-Saxon times suspected perjurers were subjected to the 'corsned', being forced to swallow consecrated barley-cake, in the belief that a lying mouth would choke on it. Later, powdered eagle-stone – a form of iron ore – was sprinkled on dry bread to see whether the accused could swallow it.

Godwine, the father of King Harold (January–October 1066), was accused of murder during the reign of Edward the Confessor and was tried by the ordeal of corsned. An ounce of bread was consecrated by exorcism, the accused was ordered to swallow it, but it stuck in Godwine's throat and he died. This practice was abolished in 1261, after the fourth Lateran Council declared it the work of the devil.

Bleeding corpse

In Scotland, if a murderer was caught red-handed, the sheriff could try the offender locally within three days. The trial was conducted by a procedure called 'bierricht' in which the accused was made to touch the corpse – if it bled, the defendant was considered to have been proved guilty. A beggar named Bell was found guilty of stabbing a neighbour at the Duke of Lauderdale's funeral in this way and was hanged in Haddington, East Lothian, in 1685. Philip Stanfield was also hanged for the murder of his father at New Mills, Haddington, in 1687, after being tried by the same method.

If, on the other hand, the corpse did not bleed, it did not necessarily mean that the accused was innocent. When in 1658 a Major Strangeways was required to touch the corpse of his murdered brother-in-law at the coroner's hearing, it did not bleed, but the case proceeded to trial anyway. Strangeways refused to plead and died by peine forte et dure – the torture of pressing the accused under heavy weights if they refused to enter a plea.

Sanctuary

If a culprit wanted to escape punishment he could claim sanctuary. Since Saxon times every church had to provide a safe haven for 40 days, after which the fugitive had to 'abjure the realm' – make their way to a seaport 'with a wooden cross in their hands, barefoot and bareheaded, in their coats only'. It was an offence to molest an abjurer who was genuinely en route out of the country. When he reached the port, if no ship was ready to take him, he had wade out into the sea up to his knees every day to show he was serious about leaving until he found passage.

Between 1478 and 1539, some 283 people accused of murder sought sanctuary in Durham. They rubbed shoulders with 16 debtors, 4 horse stealers, 9 cattle rustlers, 4 housebreakers, 7 thieves, one man charged with rape, one who had been 'backward in his accounts', one who had harboured a thief and one, curiously, who had 'failed to prosecute'.

Permanent sanctuary

Some places offered permanent sanctuary – notably the lands around the great abbeys and churches, such as Beaulieu, Westminster and St Martin-le-Grand in London, and the essentially self-governing palatines of Lancaster and Durham, and the Earldom of Chester. There the Lord Palatines had the power of a sovereign in their own domains, making and abrogating laws and appointing their own judges and courts, whose decisions they reversed if it pleased them, indicting and pardoning at their pleasure.

The centre of a sanctuary was a 'fridstool' or 'chair of peace'. Sanctuary extended for a mile around it, with the limits marked by stone crosses; once inside a criminal was safe as any infraction of the right of sanctuary invited severe penalties, including excommunication. Those who lived inside these permanent sanctuaries were called Alsatians, after the inhabitants of the disputed area between France and Germany.

One of the most famous sanctuaries was at Beverley, which had been granted its charter by King Athelstan. Near the altar of St John's was the fridstool 'to which what criminal soever flies had full protection'. Sir John Holland took sanctuary in the Church of St John at Beverley after taking revenge for the death of his squire by killing the son and heir of Hugh, the second Earl of Stafford. Holland was the half-brother of Richard II, so it was only a question of sitting it out until the King came through with a pardon.

A haven of thieves

Needless to say the system of sanctuary led to gross abuse. Even though it was decided that it should only extend to those whose punishment would involve the loss of life or limb, debtors and fraudsters also took advantage, although even those wanted on more serious charges were not always safe. In 1427, the Abbot of Beaulieu was required to give proof of his right to give sanctuary to William Wawe, reputedly a robber, highwayman, heretic and traitor. The sixteenth-century chronicler John Stow mentions merely that 'Wille Wawe was hanged'.

Even so, the permanent sanctuaries remained a haven for criminals and debtors. An account of 1500 says: 'There they build, there they spend and bid their creditors to go whistle … Thieves bring thither their stolen goods and live thereon. They devise there new robberies, nightly they steal out, they rob and steal, and kill, and come in again.'

In 1455, the Alsatians of St Martin's raided the City of London after the outbreak of the War of the Roses, and in 1487, believing wrongly that Henry VII had been beaten, they broke out and ransacked the homes of the King's followers who were away. But the sanctuary system was already under threat. The previous year Pope Innocent VIII had issued a bull relating to English sanctuaries which said that anyone who left a sanctuary's asylum lost his right of protection, even if he returned later.

From the late fifteenth century the right of sanctuary was further eroded as Henry VIII abolished the right of sanctuary for those accused of treason when in 1530 he effectively abolished the right of abjuration as too many criminals were escaping abroad. From then on, once inside a sanctuary, inmates had to stay there for life, wear a badge twenty inches long, were forbidden to carry weapons and could not leave their lodging during the hours of daylight. In 1534, ferries across the River Severn were stopped between sunrise and sunset to prevent criminals seeking refuge in the Welsh Marches. Then, in 1536, most of the palatines of the North were brought within royal writ and the dissolution of the monasteries cut down the number of places that could offer sanctuary.

In 1540, Henry ended the right of sanctuary for murder, rape, highway robbery, burglary, arson and sacrilege, although he did extend sanctuary to the cities of Wells, Manchester, Northampton, York, Derby and Launceston for minor offences. But Manchester, which was going through a cotton boom, was not at all pleased with the sudden influx of petty criminals and petitioned to have its sanctuary revoked. The petition was granted and that sanctuary – and presumably the criminals – moved to Chester.

Statutes of 1604 and 1623 removed the last legal vestiges of the sanctuary almost everywhere, but there were still a few palatine counties that maintained special sanctuaries. In Cheshire, Hoole Heath, Overmarsh, Rudheath and the abbey of Vale Royal were places of refuge. But generally the palatine county of Chester was the place of resort for those who had fallen foul of the law in other parts of the kingdom. The palatines' last privileges were eventually removed by Charles II, but other privileged places in the City of London, Westminster and Southwark were only brought within regular jurisdiction during the reigns of William III (1689–1702) and George II (1727–1760).

Swan upping

Swans have held a unique position in English law since medieval times, having been royal birds since 1186, and the only bird that can be 'estray' – that is, if they are found on common land or open water they belonged to the Crown as a prerogative right. The Crown can grant the privilege of keeping swans on open water provided they are marked and pinioned – that is, their wing feathers are removed so they can't fly. But if a bird strays and is not recaptured within a year and a day the ownership passes back to the Crown.

The swan's royal status was enshrined in statute with the Act of Swans in 1482, which introduced a right of 'possession by prescription' and a property qualification that restricted the possession of a swan mark to certain landowners to distinguish their birds. Traditionally swan marks were devices taken from the family coat of arms of the owner and cut into the upper beak with a sharp knife; they were then registered in 'swan rolls'. Once legally obtained by a grant from the Crown, these swan marks, together with the 'game of swans' marked with them, became the absolute property of the owner.

Special swanning courts known as 'swan motes' were set up to enforce the laws, with trials being presided over by a chief commissioner and decided by a jury. These courts also had the power to draw up regulations affecting swan-keeping in their area and settle disputes concerning ownership.

In 1494, Edward IV enacted 'that no one could have a game of swans' unless 'he may dispend five marks a year freehold' – the equivalent in those days to approximately £100. Later ordinances provided more regulations on the keeping and conservation of 'the kynges swanes and sygnettes', with one, the Case of Swans, dated 1592, giving credence to the myth that swans always sing before they die: 'For the cock swan is the emblem of the representation of the affectionate and true husband to his wife and about all other fowls; for the cock swan holdeth himself to one female only, and for this cause nature hath conferred on him a gift beyond all others; that is to due so joyfully, that he sings sweetly when he dies.' More recently, a specific clause was included in the Wild Creatures and Forest Law Act of 1971 to safeguard the Queen's prerogative rights over swans.

Even today there is still a 'Master of the Swans' who is responsible to the Crown for the care of the royal swans and the general supervision of swan-keeping throughout England, the post dating from at least the fourteenth century. His job was to ensure that swans were marked and pinioned, although pinioning was stopped in 1978 after pressure from animal rights organisations. And while swan marks are no longer as elaborate as they used to be, they are still considered to be cruel and unnecessary by some conservationists and animal rights activists.

Today, the swans on the River Thames have just three owners – the Queen herself and two City livery companies, the Dyers and the Vintners. The Dyers received their grant from the Crown in 1473; the Vintners around 1483. Royal swans are unmarked nowadays, so the Queen owns any strays. The Vintners' swans have a nick on each side of the beak, while the Dyers' have a single nick on one side.

The annual marking of swans is called 'swan upping', or sometimes 'swan hopping', and has been carried out on the

Thames for around 500 years, the 'upping' referring to taking the birds out of the water. Each year the number of swans is recorded and new cygnets are marked with the owner's swan mark. In the eighteenth century this became an elaborate ceremony, with specially decorated boats and the Master of Swans and his 'swan-uppers' dressed in ceremonial costumes. It used to start at London Bridge and end at Henley, but it is now restricted to the stretch of river between Walton-on-Thames and Whitchurch.

Swan upping always takes place during the third week in July when the cygnets are about a month old and are considered old enough to be handled. The Queen's Master of Swans oversees the operation and is assisted by the Swan Keepers of the Vintners and Dyers, dressed in red, white and blue uniforms. They travel in traditional wooden rowing boats, called barges, that are towed by motorboats for much of the journey as the upping has to be completed in five days. Each time a family of swans is spotted, the barges are manoeuvred so that the swans are trapped against the riverbank. The swans and cygnets are then carefully lifted out of the water and counted, the numbers are recorded and the cygnets are given the same ownership mark as the pen – that is, their mother. A naturalist is also on hand to weigh, measure and check on the health of the cygnets before the birds are returned to the water.

CHAPTER THREE

No Fun

NE OF THE PURPOSES of law is to limit fun and lead people into the paths of righteousness. This seldom works, however, for when it comes to pleasure, people will sooner or later find a way to indulge themselves, and no one has ever succeeded in legislating for virtue. But still they keep on trying.

Unlawful games

The Unlawful Games Act of 1541 banned such 'new and crafty games as logetting in the fields and slide-thrift, otherwise called shove-groat'. This hardly qualifies as the height of sin but, apparently, these games had become so popular in the houses, alleys and recreational areas of London that they were distracting men from practising archery to such an extent that 'divers bowyers and fletchers, for lack of work, had gone and inhabit themselves in Scotland and other places out of this realm, there working and teaching their science to the puis-

sance [power] of the same, to the great comfort of estrangers and the detriment of this realm'.

The Act aimed to crack down on this and made it illegal for foreigners to use a longbow; nor were foreigners allowed to export bows and arrows. Meanwhile every Englishman between 17 and 60 who was not lame, decrepit or maimed, a priest, a justice or a 'baron of the exchequer' had to keep a longbow and arrows in his house and practise shooting. Any man who had a 'man-child' between the ages of seven and 17 in his house had to keep a bow and two shafts to teach the boy archery. If the boy was a servant, the price of the bow and arrows could be deducted from his wages. Once the boy reached 17, he had to provide the bow and arrows himself.

The Act also required magistrates to stop unlawful games and close down the houses where they were played. Although any nobleman whose property was worth more than £100 a year was allowed to permit his servants to play 'cards, dice, tables, bowls or tennis … within the precincts of their houses, gardens or orchards', these games were banned for craftsmen.

Game cocks in school

In the City of London in the twelfth century, it was the custom for boys to take their gamecocks to school on Shrove Tuesday. They would turn their schoolroom into cockpits and spend the morning watching cockfights. Schoolroom cockfighting continued in Congleton, Cheshire, until at least 1601, and in Scotland schoolboys continued their annual cockfights until as late as the nineteenth century.

Cockfighting was only banned in England in 1849, but a similar Act for Scotland, known as the Cruelty to Animals (Scotland) Act, was not passed because it made no mention of game- or fighting-cocks. It was only in May 1895 that it was amended, adding to the definition of 'animals' in the Act 'any game- or fighting-cock, or other domestic fowl or bird'.

Don't roll out the barrel

The Metropolitan Police Act of 1839 prohibits the rolling of 'any cask, tub, hoop, or wheel … on any footway, except for the purpose of loading or unloading any cart or carriage'.

The public are not allowed to feed or shoe horses on the carriageway, though they can herd cattle along the streets, provided they do not 'wantonly and unlawfully pelt, drive or hunt any such cattle'.

At that time bear-baiting and cockfighting were still going on and the Metropolitan Police Act stipulated that anyone keeping a place for the 'fighting or baiting of lions, bears, badgers, cocks, docks or other animals' was liable to a fine of up to £5, with up to one month in gaol with or without hard labour.

Like much of the 1839 Act, this section is still in force – though there is no record of anyone being so foolhardy as to bait a bear within the Metropolitan district recently.

Under the same Act, children are not allowed to fly a kite 'or play at any game to the annoyance of the inhabitants'. Nor can they 'slide upon ice or snow', set off fireworks, build bonfires, ring doorbells 'without lawful excuse, or … wilfully extinguish the light of any lamp'.

Drunkenness

The Drunkenness Act of 1606 could have been written yesterday, for it begins:

> Whereas the loathsome and odious sin of drunkenness is of late grown into common use within this realm, being the root and foundation of many other enormous sins, as bloodshed, stabbing, murder, swearing, fornication, adultery and such like, to the great dishonour of God, and of our nation, the overthrow of many good arts and manual trades, the disabling of divers workmen and the general impoverishment of many good subjects, abusively wasting the good creatures of God.

Under the Act, drunks were to be fined five shillings – 25p – or spend six hours in the stocks. Perhaps because Members of Parliament were among the most frequent offenders in this arena, the law did not come into force until 'forty days next following the end of this present session of parliament' – which would have given MPs enough time to sober up.

Constables or other officers of the parish who neglected to arrest drunks – perhaps because they were drunk themselves – were fined ten shillings (50p). Publicans who allowed drunks to 'remain drinking or tippling' were also fined ten shillings, but then the landlord would be fined 20 shillings for selling less than a quart of best beer or ale for a penny by the 1604 Act to restrain the inordinate Haunting and Tippling in Inns, Ale-houses and other Victualling-houses. Offenders themselves would be fined another 3s 4d – 17p – or spend four hours in the stocks. They could also be punished by the ecclesiastical courts, especially if any adultery or fornication resulted due to their drunkenness, as it so often does.

Fortunately for the students, the 1606 Act, like the 1604 Act before it, did not apply in the universities. It remains, of course, illegal to sell, attempt to sell or allow alcohol to be sold to someone who is drunk, not least under the Licensing Act of 2003.

In medieval times drunkards were made to walk around town wearing wooden barrels with holes for their heads and arms. This was called a 'drunkard's cloak' and was designed to shame the culprit into sobriety. Before the 1604 Act introduced fines, the stocks were the standard punishment for drunkards – in 1500 Cardinal Wolsey, then a priest in Limington, near Yeovil, was put in the stocks for drunkenness.

Licensing Act

The Licensing Act of 1872 once again made it unlawful to be drunk in a pub or bar and the Criminal Justice and Police Act of 2001 gave the police the right to collect a fine on the spot from anyone drunk on licensed premises – any shortage in the constabulary budget can surely be made up on a Saturday night.

But while the constabulary coffers may now be bulging, Section 16 of the 1872 Act fined licencees for supplying liquor or refreshment to a police constable on duty, although the Act thoughtfully made provision for constables, superintendents and justices of the peace to enter licensed premises after closing time.

In the cooler

A thirsty policeman might be better off in prison. While Sir Robert Peel's Gaols (England) Act of 1823 banned 'spirituous liquors, or wine of any kind, cider or perry', relief was at hand. Another clause maintained that: 'No beer shall be admitted to the prison, except between the hours of twelve and one on weekdays, and between two and half-past two on Sundays, Christmas Day and Good Friday.' But you would need a pint to wash down the prison food stipulated by the Act, which fixed the prisoner's daily ration at 'twenty-four ounces of good wheaten bread, sixteen ounces of potatoes, four ounces of oatmeal and a quarter of an ounce of salt'. The Act also stipulated: 'No gaming shall be permitted in the prison and the keeper shall seize and destroy all cards, dice or other instruments of gaming.'

Sunday bloody Sunday

Until the Sunday Trading Act of 1994, what you could and could not do on a Sunday was regulated by the Sunday Observance Act of 1781. This Act made it illegal to take money as an entrance fee to places of entertainment, effectively banning sporting events such as football, boxing and wrestling matches. Neither were you allowed to charge more for refreshments at venues, in lieu of an entrance fee, which affected variety shows, circuses and 'public dancing'. It was also illegal to advertise 'public amusements' on a Sunday in order to prevent the 'corruption of good morals, to the great encouragement of irreligion and profaneness'.

It was not until the Sunday Theatre Act of 1972 that these restrictions were lifted for stage performances and even today, the hours during which plays can be performed are limited on Sundays.

At least the 1625 law banning 'bear-baiting, bull-baitings, enterludes, common plays and all other unlawful exercises and pastimes on the Lord's Day' was repealed in 1969. Enterludes were originally short comic episodes that appeared between the acts of morality plays which had developed into popular farces during the seventeenth century. The fine for staging such wicked entertainment on Sunday was 3s 4d (17p).

Under the Shops Act of 1950, *Playboy* and *Penthouse* magazines could be purchased on the Sabbath, though the Bible could not. Shopkeepers who ignored this statute could be fined as much as £25, although this too has been repealed and everyone can now enjoy both erotica and the word of the Lord on the Sabbath.

In Manchester there was a bye-law that forced every city councillor to attend church on Sunday, while in Somerset there was a bye-law maintaining that people were not to wear the same clothes on Sunday as they did during the rest of the week.

Censorship

Censorship was traditionally the job of the Catholic Church with its Index of Proscribed Books, but when Henry VIII split with Rome, he took over the task. His first attempt at censorship was the Religion Act of 1542, which banned the Bible or any other religious work that had been translated into English. The Act also stated: 'No person shall play in enterlude, sing or rhime, contrary to the said doctrine.' The punishment for a first offence was to recant, 'for his second to abjure and bear a faggot, and for his third shall be adjudged an heretic and be burned and lose all his goods and chattels'. To bear a faggot meant that the offender was burned – but at least he didn't lose his belongings. This Act was repealed in 1547 and by 1611 James I had published his own Authorised version of the Bible in English.

In 1637 a more systematic approach to censorship was taken by the Court of the Star Chamber, a court of senior judges and privy councillors that enforced the King's prerogative and sat without a jury. It decreed that all books should be licensed by the Archbishop of Canterbury, who was later required to fix the price of books, or the Bishop of London – as if they had time for all that reading. The Star Chamber was abolished by puritans of the Long Parliament, which sat from 1640 until 1653, who passed several Acts of their own restricting publishing.

Censorship continued after the Restoration. Under the

Licensing of the Press Act of 1662, no book was to be published until it was licensed, registered with Stationers' Hall and, curiously, the consent of the author had been obtained. But in 1692, it was discovered that the official censor had, inadvertently, licensed a book – *The History of the Bloody Assizes* – which the House of Commons had said should be burned by the public hangman. The censor, a man named Bohun, was promptly imprisoned, which made the Act a laughing stock and it was not renewed. Obscenity laws stayed in force, however, until the trial involving D.H. Lawrence's *Lady Chatterley's Lover* in 1960 forced a change in the law.

Critics

Although an author can escape the judgement of the Church, the courts and the censor, he cannot escape the judgement of critics. The nineteenth-century Chief Justice Lord Ellenborough ruled that there should be no limit to the contempt and ridicule that could be heaped on a book, provided that the critic does not 'introduce fiction for the purpose of condemnation' or 'impute fraud, immorality, corruption or something bordering on crime that might merit a libel action'. In the case he was judging, the author had complained that a tasteless satirical cartoon lampooning him had made his book unsaleable and had lost him a publisher for a forthcoming work.

The theatre

The Plays Act of 1605 banned plays that mocked God, Christ, the Holy Ghost or the Trinity and under the puritanical rule of the Commonwealth, the theatre was banned altogether, although with the Restoration of Charles II, it was soon in action again.

In 1713, actors, being feckless individuals, fell foul of the Vagrants Act. However, in the reigns of George II and George III, the law was amended, allowing theatres to obtain licences so that plays could be put on again, and London theatres were specifically excluded from the Disorderly Houses Act of 1751. However, the Plays Act of 1736 required that new plays, including operas and pantomimes, be submitted to the Lord Chamberlain. The Theatres Act of 1843 extended the law to dialogues between two people in costume, but not 'theatrical representations as are given in booths or shows allowed by the justices at fairs and feasts'. The role of the Lord Chamberlain in the theatre continued until 1968, when it was abolished by a new Theatres Act.

Bonfire night

The same year that the first Plays Act was passed, Guy Fawkes was discovered trying to blow up the King and the Houses of Parliament in the ill-fated Gunpowder Plot. As a result the Observance of 5th November Act was passed, which required the people of England to celebrate 'with unfeigned thank fulness ... this joyful day of deliverance' as a 'perpetual remembrance ... for all ages to come'. This meant that you were supposed to go to church where prayers of thanksgiving were to be said, 'and there to abide orderly and soberly at the time of the said prayers, preaching or other service of God'. This law making it compulsory to celebrate the arrest of Guy Fawkes stayed in force in England and its Dominions until 1859.

However, there is one law concerning bonfire night still in force which says it is only permissible for children to go door to door collecting 'a penny for the guy' with the written permission of the local chief constable of police – no mention of 'trick or treat' on Halloween without his consent.

Burning books

Bonfires of books and other publications condemned by the House of Commons as seditious were common until 1763. The burning was usually done by the public hangman in Palace Yard at 1.00 p.m., although the Commons had such contempt for the radical John Wilkes's attack on the King's speech in issue No. 45 of the *North Briton* that they did not want to dignify it by burning it in Westminster, and ordered that it be incinerated in Cheapside in the City.

When the sheriff tried to carry out the order, his officials were pelted with stones by the crowd who cried: 'Wilkes and liberty.' So the sheriff's men burned a petticoat and some

jackboots instead. Parliament was so deeply disturbed by this that an enquiry was set up that went on for four days, and no attempt has been made to burn anything publicly since then.

Malicious damage

Whereas Parliament is still technically allowed to burn books, others are not. Section 39 of the Malicious Damage Act of 1861 states:

> Whoever shall unlawfully and maliciously destroy or damage any book, manuscript, picture, print, statue, bust or vase, or any other article or thing kept for the purpose of art, science or literature, or as repository … either at all times for from time to time open for the admission of the public … shall be guilty of misdemeanour, and, being convicted thereof, shall be liable to be imprisoned for any term not exceeding six months, with or without hard labour; and if a male under the age of sixteen years, with or without whipping; provided that nothing herein contained shall be deemed to affect the right of any person to recover by action at law damages for the injuries so committed.

It was for this offence that the playwright Joe Orton and his lover (and later, murderer) Kenneth Halliwell, were gaoled for six months in 1962.

Public meetings

The right to hold a public meeting is relatively new and throughout most of English history unauthorised public gatherings were held to be seditious. However, on 29 August 1769, the electors of Westminster gathered in Westminster Hall to adopt a petition for the redress of their grievances. After the radical John Wilkes was expelled from the House of Commons the following year they became more frequent and Parliament tried to ban them. In a heated debate, a law officer told the House of Commons that England was the only country in the world where such a meeting could take place without the attendance of a magistrate, and pointed out that even ancient Rome 'in the zenith of its liberty' did not allow such things.

Although it was generally conceded that public meetings had put an end to the American War of Independence, the Seditious Meetings Act was passed in 1819. This limited the size of any meeting to 50 people and legislated that the organisers must give six days' notice of the event. But there was an unexpected loophole – while it was all very well to pass an Act limiting meetings in public places, in London the royal parks belong to the Crown, so are, in fact, private property. In 1856, law officers informed the government that they could only eject people from the royal parks using the laws of trespass, which meant they could not use unreasonable force to make people leave if they refused to do so, as manhandling them would constitute assault. Nor could the police order a meeting to disperse – people could only be removed from private property if notice of their eviction was given to each of them individually.

In recognition of this, the Parks Regulation Act was passed in 1872, setting aside an area within each park for public meetings, one of which was Speakers' Corner in Hyde Park. Meanwhile the Seditious Meetings Act was no longer used but was not repealed until 1986.

Tumultuous petition

Although people could speak out as much as they liked in the park, they could not take their grievances to anyone in authority. The Tumultuous Petitioning Act of 1661 had made it illegal to gather more than 20 people to petition, complain to or otherwise address the King or either Houses of Parliament for the 'alternation of matters established by law in church or state' unless the consent of three justices of the peace or the majority of a grand jury was first obtained. The public were not even allowed to approach the King or Parliament with more than ten people, without incurring a fine of £100 and three months in gaol. This Act was not revised until as recently as 1948 before being finally repealed in 1986.

CHAPTER FOUR

The Laws that Never Were

 HE STATUS OF THE LAWS passed during the Civil War, and the Commonwealth that followed, is unclear. The Law Society maintains that the laws passed between the time Charles I fell out with Parliament in 1640 and the return of Charles II to England in 1660 are not in force because they were not signed into law by a king. However, in January 1649, Parliament abolished the office of king, so the laws it passed did not need his assent – although as that Act itself did not get the royal assent it could be considered unlawful. A committee of the House of Commons decided that it would be better not to try and confirm or deny the status of these laws – indeed, they could not be denied as some of them had already had consequences that could not be undone; and they could not be confirmed as there was the small matter of the Act of 17 March 1649, which declared that it was high treason for anyone to adopt the 'name, style, dignity, power, prerogative or authority of king of England and Ireland'. This would have made Charles II – and, indeed, our own dear Queen – a traitor, so it was simply better to pretend that the interregnum never existed. In volume seven of *The Statutes at Large*, the laws of 1640 end on page 358 and the laws of 1660 begin on page 359, with no sign of the laws passed in between. Whereas some provisions of the Commonwealth were deliberated voided by subsequent Acts, others were confirmed – there was even an Act legitimising all marriages conducted during the interregnum.

Many unpopular Acts signed by Cromwell were destroyed at the Restoration, so disappeared in fact, if not in law. It was not until 1899 that the Statute Law Committee began to recompile them from printed copies and other sources, and the resulting *Acts and Ordinances of the Interregnum* appeared in print in three volumes in 1911.

Mince pies

During the interregnum Cromwell introduced a law banning mince pies at Christmas. It is said that this was done because the ingredients of mince pies and plum puddings were pagan in origin, and their consumption was part of an ancient fertility ritual, along with maypoles, dancing in church, yule logs and decorating the home with holly and ivy – all of which is not true.

In 1642, a law was passed decreeing a fast on the last Wednesday of every month, but in 1644, Christmas fell on the last Wednesday in December and it was unclear to people whether they should feast or fast. So the Puritans passed a special law confirming that a fast should be held on Christmas Day, which should be observed with 'more solemn humiliation, because it may call to remembrance our sins and the sins of our forefathers, who have turned this feast, pretending the memory of Christ, into an extreme forgetfulness of him by giving liberty to carnal and sensual delights, contrary to the life which Christ himself led here on Earth'.

The dispute over mince pies may have arisen because importing currants was banned in 1642, which may have curbed the festive endeavours of the pastry chefs of the Commonwealth, who could have substituted raisins, which were not banned. The reason for this was that currants came from Islamic Turkey, while raisins came from Christian Greece. At the time, though, mince pies contained mincemeat, so the unavailability of a particular fruit should not have been a problem.

For good measure the Puritans abolished all other feast days, but allowed servants, scholars and apprentices to have the second Tuesday of every month off for recreation and relaxation.

Pleasing God

On 26 August 1643, an Act was passed for the destruction of all altars and communion tables, along with 'tapers, candlesticks … crucifixes, crosses, and all images and pictures of any one or more persons of the Trinity, or of the Virgin Mary, all other images and pictures of saints, or superstitious inscriptions' in churches, chapels, other places of public prayers and churchyards. These were to be destroyed along with altar rails, the ground where altars had stood was to be levelled and stained-glass windows were to be smashed. The Puritans were so fanatical about this that they passed another Act on 9 May 1644, ordering the same thing once again, along with the destruction of any frames or cases where images stood, all organs and 'all copes, surplisses, superstitious vestments, roods and fonts' – to 'please God'. And yet images of kings, princes, noblemen and knights, along with their coats of arms, were allowed to remain.

The play's not the thing

Although plays were suppressed in 1642 for being 'spectacles of pleasure, too commonly expressing lascivious mirth and levity', theatrical people are surprisingly resilient and were still going about their business in October 1647 when the Lord Mayor, justices of the peace, the sheriffs of the City of London and Westminster, and the counties of Middlesex and Surrey were given authority to enter any establishment where they thought a play was being performed. Actors were to be arrested, gaoled and 'punished as rogues according to law', which meant that if they did not give up their profession immediately, they would be banished or sent to the gallows.

When even this did not stop them, a new Act was passed in February 1648. This time actors were to be whipped publicly, before being banished or sent to the gallows, which would have been a performance in itself. The box office takings were to be forfeited to the Church and the audience were fined five shillings – 25p – each time they had attended a performance. The Act also called for the demolition of all stages, galleries, boxes and seats, and the buildings they were in were to be destroyed.

Fornication

The Act of the Suppressing of the Detestable Sins of Incest, Adultery and Fornication of 10 May 1650 prevented anyone marrying or having carnal knowledge of 'his or her grandfather or grandmother, father or mother, brother or sister, son or daughter, or grandchild, father's brother or sister, mother's brother or sister, father's wife, mother's husband, son's wife, daughter's husband, wife's mother or daughter, husband's father or son'. All these relationships were declared incestuous and adjudged a felony which attracted the death penalty without benefit of clergy.

The Act also proscribed adultery where 'any married woman ... be carnally known by any man (other than her husband) (except in case of ravishment)'. This too was a felony, punishable by death without benefit of clergy, although there were mitigating circumstances. It did not include 'any man who, at the time of such offence committed, is not knowing that such a woman with whom such offence is committed, is then married'. Nor did it apply to

> any woman whose husband shall be remaining beyond the seas by the space of three years, or shall by common fame be reputed to be dead; nor to any woman whose husband shall absent himself from his said wife by the space of three years together, in any parts or places whatsoever, so as the said wife shall not know her said husband to be living within that time.

This is remarkably liberal as Drake's circumnavigation of the world 70 years before took just three months short of three years.

A man who seduced a virgin, an unmarried woman or a widow was gaoled for three months. The woman concerned suffered the same punishment and both of them had to promise to be of good behaviour for the following year.

Men or women who were 'common bawds', or who knowingly kept brothels or bawdy houses, would be whipped for

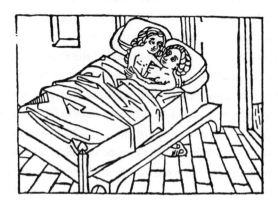

their first offence, put in the pillory, branded with the letter 'B' on their forehead and sent to gaol for three years; a second offence attracted the death penalty without benefit of clergy. At least there was no attainder so the culprit's property was not confiscated and the children could keep any inheritance.

'The detestable and abominable vice of buggery committed with mankind or beast', 'all rapes and carnal ravishment of women', including marrying 'any maid, widow or damsel' against her will, 'procuring or abetting any such ravishment', marrying again before a former wife or husband was dead, and 'all offences of invocations, conjurations, witchcrafts, sorceries, enchantments and charms' were excluded from a general pardon of 1652.

Swearing

During the interregnum swearing was banned, penalties being 30 shillings for a lord, 20 shillings for a baronet or a knight, 6s 8d for a gentleman and 3s 4d for 'all inferiors'; the fine was doubled for a second offence. Failure to pay up would earn the offender three hours in the stocks or, if they were under the age of 12, a whipping. For a tenth offence, the perpetrator, irrespective of rank or status, would be adjudged a 'Common Swearer or Curser' and be bound with 'sureties to good behaviour'. If the bad language continued the culprit's goods and chattels would be seized and sold, any default in payment earning six hours in the stocks. Under a law of 1650, if a woman was arrested for swearing the penalty would have to be paid by her husband or, in the case of a widow or single woman, her father.

The word of God

'Abominable blasphemies and damnable heresies' were seen as such a problem that Parliament set aside Wednesday, 10 March 1647 as a 'day of public humiliation'. When that did not work a law was passed on 2 May 1648 making denying the Trinity, or doubting that the books of Habakkuk, Zephaniah, Haggai, Zecharia and Malachi in the Old Testament were not the word of God, punishable by death, without benefit of clergy. And to prevent such scandalous ideas being spread, printing presses were only allowed in the City of London and the universities of Oxford and Cambridge, where the Company of Stationers could keep an eye on them.

There were other doctrinal errors to beware of. For example, maintaining that 'man by nature hath free will', or that 'God may be worshipped in or by pictures or images', or that 'man is bound to believe no more than by his reason he can comprehend' were 'heinous errors', punishable by imprisonment.

The law that never was

There is another law that never was. During the short reign of Richard III he signed an Act bastardising all the children of his older brother Edward IV. It was never repealed. Instead it was ripped from the files of the Chancery and burned, on the advice of all the judges in England, so that 'no memory might remain of it'.

CHAPTER FIVE

Sexual Strictures

 HERE ARE FEW THINGS people in authority enjoy more than devising strange laws concerning other people's sex lives. Not only are the statute books bulging with laws on adultery, fornication and buggery, but Church elders, judges, justices of the peace and local authorities like to get in on the act too. With so many pieces of statute law, bye-law, ecclesiastical law and case law, it is almost impossible to discover in what circumstance they came about and whether they are still in force. Some, indeed, may be apocryphal.

The art of adultery

In pre-Saxon early British history adultery did not seem to be a problem – wives could be shared between groups of 10 or 12 men. Indeed, it was not uncommon for brothers to share their wives, and sometimes fathers and sons shared the same women – if the woman bore any children, the father was considered to be the man with whom she had cohabited first.

However, during the Saxon era, laws against adultery were introduced – the co-respondent was automatically sentenced to hang, while the unfaithful spouse was tied to a stake and burned alive; the woman's ashes were then scattered under the gallows where her lover's body dangled. The Danes on the other hand were less even handed – King Canute decreed that any woman caught in the act had her nose and both ears cut off, while the guilty male was merely banished from the country.

During the reign of Henry I, adulterers were first castrated and then blinded, while a wife was expected to be faithful after the death of her husband. Under the Crown Forfeitures Act of 1324, a woman who commited fornication in her widowhood, or took another husband, forfeited her dowry to the Crown.

The price of adultery

Until as recently as 1973 it was possible for a husband to claim damages from his wife's lover if she was unfaithful to him. In the quaint wording of the Matrimonial Causes Act of 1857, the wife and her lover were said to have engaged in 'criminal

conversation'. A wronged wife could also sue, although before the Law Reform (Married Women and Tortfeasors) Act of 1935, if a married woman seduced the husband of another and the injured wife sued, if she won, the damages had to be paid by the seducer's husband.

Buggery

During the reign of Richard I – widely thought to have indulged in it himself – those convicted of sodomy were hanged, burned, stoned to death, buried alive or drowned.

Henry VIII passed a Buggery Act and his son Edward VI passed a Sodomy Act for good measure. Then in 1562 Elizabeth I again banned the 'detestable vice of buggery', after her sister Mary had legalised it in the first year of her reign 'to the high displeasure of Almighty God'. Elizabeth's attorney-general Sir Edward Coke said in court, 'Buggery is a detestable and abominable sin, amongst Christians not to be named, committed by mankind with mankind, or with brute beast, or by womankind with brute beast.'

In sixteen-century England it was punishable by burning at the stake or hanging, and it carried the death penalty until 1861, but since then, the law has become considerably more lenient. The Sexual Offences Act of 1967 legalised homosexual acts for consenting adult males in private, provided they weren't members of the armed forces, although buggery is still illegal for heterosexuals. But there is a loophole here – under the Sexual Offences Act of 1956, a wife cannot testify against her husband in a buggery case, unless the person on the receiving end is under 17.

The love that dare not speak its name

The Criminal Law Amendment Act of 1885 made 'gross indecency' between members of the same sex a punishable offence, but when the bill was presented to Queen Victoria, she was supposed to have said, 'Women don't do such things,' so any reference to lesbianism was removed.

In another version of the story, lesbianism was excluded from the bill because no one was willing to explain it to the Queen.

Whatever the case, the resulting law only refers to men. The clause in question states:

> Any male person who, in public or private, commits, or is party to the commission of, or procures or attempts to procure the commission by any male person of, any act of gross indecency with another male person, shall be guilty of a misdemeanour, and being convicted thereof shall be liable at the discretion of the court to be imprisoned for any term not exceeding two years, with or without hard labour.

This is the provision Oscar Wilde fell foul of in 1895. Curiously, the full title of the Act is 'An Act to make further provision for the Protection of Women and Girls, the suppression of brothels, and other purposes'.

Dress codes

Lesbianism was by no means unknown in England – an Act of 1777 banned any woman from 'disguising herself in men's clothing and courting other women', the sentence for which was six months imprisonment, with several appearances in the pillory.

Queen Anne – a well-known follower of Sappho herself – banned women from wearing masks to the theatre, something ladies did in order to remain incognito while watching bawdy plays. But by the beginning of the eighteenth century it seems that prostitutes had taken to using the same device to slip unnoticed into theatres and solicit for trade between acts.

Gratuitous nudity

James I passed a topless Act, under the provisions of which young women were not to be seen in public unless their breasts were exposed to the nipple. At the time this was taken as a symbol of their virginity.

Such exposure would not be a problem in Whitehaven, Cumbria, where women are permitted to walk around with their breasts bared. A seaside resort, it attracts its share of topless sunbathers, so the local constabulary looked into the matter and found nothing in law that compelled women to cover their breasts. 'If they want to just walk down the street topless, that's their privilege,' said a spokesperson.

Liverpool is supposed to be the home of other strange laws concerning nudity. It is said, for example, to be unlawful to 'dress or undress a female mannequin in the window of any store or shop where children might observe the unclothed model'. The same ordinance is also said to forbid any child 'peering up the dress of a mannequin'. If it happens, the parents are held responsible and can be arrested.

Streaking is against the law, but although exponents are technically guilty of 'indecent exposure', they are rarely prosecuted. According to the Home Office Committee: 'Streakers are looked upon as no more than relatively innocent pranksters. They are presently able to avoid any stigma or a conviction for indecent exposure.'

Metrosexual

In an effort to cut down on 'molly houses' – homosexual brothels – in London in the sixteenth century, it became illegal for two adult men to have sex in the same house as a third person.

According to an old City ordinance, it is against the law to check into a hotel in London under assumed names for the purpose of lovemaking, the fine for 'falsifying a hotel registration' to obtain a room for sex rather than sleeping being £20. It is also illegal to make love in trains, buses, parked cars, churchyards, churches or parks.

This is sadly at odds with the teachings of the Good Book, or one edition of it at least. In 1631, an authorised edition of the Bible was printed in London with the key word 'not' missing, thereby turning the stern Seventh Commandment into the exhortation: 'Thou shalt commit adultery'. Its printers, Robert Barker and Martin Lucas, were fined £3,000 and the so-called 'Wicked Bible' became a much sought-after item.

Regional romps

When topless go-go dancers began appearing in clubs in the 1960s, Birmingham City Council tried to curb the trend and passed ordinance requiring all go-go dancers to wear bras while performing on stage. Later the law later was amended when the council said that it 'recognised there were differences between men and women'. 'In future,' a spokesman said, 'no male go-go dancer will hereafter have to wear a brassiere.'

Couples must also be careful what they do after they leave a club or pub. Under an old city ordinance in Birmingham it was illegal for a man and a woman to have sex 'on the steps of any church after the sun goes down'. Getting caught in the act brings a charge of 'disorderly conduct' and risks a fine of up to £25 each – although it seems there was no law against doing it in daylight.

A wife and mother

In Hertford, a wife has the right to throw out her husband's collection of girlie magazines, blue movies and any other material of a sexual nature that he has stashed away. While in

Nottingham, it is illegal for a woman to use her wiles on a man to break up his family – an old law states that a woman cannot 'fraudulently and deceitfully' lure a single man away from his mother in order to bring about a 'clandestine marriage'.

'Advertising, not soliciting'

When a 26-year-old prostitute in Southampton was arrested on a charge of soliciting – she had been posing seductively in a window lit by a red light, but not on the street – a local magistrate ruled that the woman was 'advertising, not soliciting' and dismissed all the charges.

Bristol fashion

In Bristol, lovers are not allowed to kick a dog out of bed if it gets in the way during intercourse as apparently a dog – but not a cat – has the right to be a voyeur. However, if it tries to join it, one of the human participants might risk committing a felony under the 1956 Sexual Offences Act.

It seems there is another strange bye-law concerning sex in Bristol, where couples are banned from making love while lying under a car – they can do it inside the vehicle if they wish, but the law specifically bans having sex underneath it.

Driving passion

There are a number of other strange laws concerning sex and automobiles. It seems that if a man takes a woman out for a drive in Leeds on a Sunday, he is forbidden to make any suggestion of an amorous nature to her while he is behind the wheel. This law applies specifically to cars as it is perfectly proper for a man to ask his lady friend for her sexual favours if he is driving a bus, truck, van or tractor.

Drivers in and around Leighton Buzzard, Bedfordshire, are not allowed to kiss a passenger while cruising down 'winding roads'. If they do, both driver and passenger can be fined, although it is, apparently, safe to kiss on a straight road.

Couples in Edinburgh are banned from having sex in vehicles parked in car parks or on public streets. However, it seems they are allowed to make love when their car is parked on their own property – providing they do so on the back seat.

Sex in Scotland

From the Scottish Reformation in 1560 to the beginning of the twentieth century, members of the Church of Scotland and of the Free Church of Scotland could be summoned before the Session and called to answer charges of sexual impropriety. If found guilty they could be struck off the Kirk roll, and reinstated if they publicly admitted their guilt and married.

The Kirk has now relaxed its grip, but some strange practices linger on. Montrose, for example, has an ordinance banning copulation by animals – both household animals and livestock – in any public place within the city limits. The owner of any animal found breaking this law can be thrown in gaol for up to 25 days and fined up to £15.

In Dundee, unmarried couples were prohibited from going to one another's homes to make love – indeed they were banned from going unchaperoned to any private place for purposes of immorality.

More adventurous forms of sex are still frowned on. When a young woman was arrested in Dumbarton for having sex with two men, she was charged with 'lewd and lascivious conduct', fined £300 and had her name and address published in the local paper.

Tossing the caber

Couples who apply for a marriage licence in Paisley are given a booklet on contraception to study – and are then tested on it before the licence is issued.

In Dumfries, it is against the law for any person to 'entice or allure, instigate or aid any person under eighteen to commit masturbation or self-pollution'. Both men and women can be prosecuted and sent to gaol.

And it seems that the Scots are all too easily aroused. In Hollybush, South Ayrshire, it is illegal to display condoms and other contraceptives in a chemists where they could be seen young customers. A local bye-law states that such 'sexually stimulating' items cannot be openly displayed as they might 'encourage promiscuity'.

First footing

Scotland's strange sex laws stretch right back to the eleventh century. After killing Macbeth and seizing the crown of Scotland, Malcolm III set about modernising the old feudal system by curbing the old maiden rights, or droit de seigneur, whereby the lord of the manor got first crack at the bride before her wedding, by putting it on a more businesslike footing – the maiden could pay a quit-rent to save her virginity for her husband. But the laird still symbolically asserted his right to her maidenhead by thrusting a booted foot into the couple's bed on their wedding night, or casting the bridegroom into a stream.

Aye do

Until the passing of the Marriage (Scotland) Act of 1939, if a man seduced a woman by promising to marry her, the act of intercourse itself was deemed to constitute matrimony and the knot was legally tied. The 1939 Act abolished what was known in Scotland as marriage *subsequente copula*.

Welshing in Wales

The strange compensation given to a Welsh maiden who had been welshed on by her boyfriend is recorded in the book *Welsh Medieval Law*. In a section on Worthynbury in Flintshire, it says:

The recompence to a virgin, who had been seduced, is very singular: on complaint made that she was deserted by her lover, it was ordered by the court that she was to lay hold of the tail of a bull of three years old, introduced through a wicker door, and shaven and well greased. Two men were to goad the beast: if she could, by dint of strength, retain the bull, she was to have it by way of satisfaction; if not, she got nothing but the grease that remained on her hands.

Bastardy

Sex laws are strictest when children are born as a result – in feudal times it was better to be born out of wedlock. The son of a serf automatically belonged to his father's master, but a bastard was a *filius nullius* – the son of nobody – and therefore a free man, although it was necessary to get a certificate from the local bishop stating that you were a bastard.

Until the reign of Edward IV, if you were born before your parents married, you would be legitimate under ecclesiastical law but a bastard under common law.

The Bastardy Act of 1575 compelled all women pregnant with an illegitimate child to identify the father. The man was then arrested and faced a simple choice – marriage or prison. This was repealed by the Poor Law Amendment Act of 1834.

An Act of 1743–1744 required an illegitimate child's place of settlement to be the mother's place of origin, regardless of where she gave birth. The mother could also be punished by means of a public whipping. An Act of 1810 went even further. Under it, a woman pregnant with a 'baseborn child' could be sentenced to between six and 12 months in a house of correction – and perhaps even be made to stay there until she showed signs of reform.

These days there is no disgrace in illegitimacy, except in the eyes of the Church of England. Anyone about to be ordained as a deacon in the C of E is required to give proof that they are not a bastard. If that is not possible, they can apply to the Archbishop of Canterbury, who can grant dispensation. Once granted the candidate can go on to be a deacon and even a priest – but not a bishop.

Marriage post mortem?

The full majesty of the law has been brought to bear on the marriage rights of the newly dead. In the 1700s, a young woman, forsaken by a lover who had previously promised to marry her, died, perhaps of a broken heart. The executors of her will then sued her faithless suitor for breach of promise and won damages. When the lover appealed in an attempt to get his money back, the case was heard by Lord Ellenborough, who decided that although marriage 'may be considered a temporal advantage to the party, as far as respects personal comfort', marital bliss was not part of a person's 'transmissible personal estate'. He reversed the judgement, deciding that 'the young lady's executor cannot receive damages for breach of promise.'

No sex after marriage

In 1931, a man sought to have his marriage annulled because, after 14 years of trying, his wife was incapable of consummating the union. But his petition was refused. Even though the court believed his story, the judge said, 'In the course of this very unhappy married life, he had more success than he imagines.'

In 1778 a woman was refused an annulment on the grounds that her husband was impotent. Relating the report of medical inspectors who had examined the man's seemingly flaccid member, the judge told the court: 'They could only say it appeared soft and short, which does not always continue.'

But some people are just plain greedy. A 30-year-old British mechanic filed a suit for divorce from his American wife on the grounds that she did not give him enough sex. His petition was denied because, in the words of the judge: 'It seems quite impossible for any court to find that the refusal of a wife to have sex more often than once a week is unreasonable.'

Previous pre-nuptials

There is nothing new about pre-nuptial agreements. In 1867, a porter named William Pritchard Dragg married Catherine Jeffries, a cook in a hospital, who was carrying his child. Before the ceremony they signed an agreement which read:

This is to certify that whereas the unsigned parties do agree that they will marry, and that only to save the female of us from shaming her friends or telling a lie, and that the said marriage shall be no more thought of, except to tell her friends that she was married (unless she should arrive at the following accomplishments – viz., piano, singing, reading, writing, speaking and deportment); and whereas these said accomplishments have in no way been sought after, much less mastered, therefore the aforesaid marriage shall be and is null and void; and whereas we agree that the male of us shall keep the harmonium in the aforesaid female's sitting room, we agree that it shall be there no more than four months, and that from that time the aforesaid and undersigned shall be free in every respect whatsoever if the aforesaid and undersigned female, as witnessed by our hands.

Fifteen years later, in 1882, Dagg sought a divorce from Catherine on the grounds of adultery. According to the court report: 'A month after the marriage the respondent was delivered of a child, at a lodging taken for her by the petitioner; but he had no further intercourse with her. He paid her 2s 6d a week until recently, when he discovered that she had been for some years living in adultery with another man.'

Dagg's divorce petition was refused on the grounds that, having got her pregnant outside marriage in the first place, he had 'known her frailty', consequently 'it was his duty, when he became her husband, not to have left her to those chances of falling, to which, abandoned as she was by him, she must have been exposed … He withdrew from her that protection to which, as his wife, she was entitled, and it is not to be wondered at that she fell with another man.'

1891 Slander of Women Act

It is still an offence under this act to 'impute unchastity or adultery' to any woman in England, Wales or Ireland. The law does not apply in Scotland, presumably because the men wear skirts up there and it would be too confusing.

CHAPTER SIX

Diet and Apparel

 AWMAKERS LIKE TO INTERFERE with what people wear and what they eat and drink, often saying that this is for their own good – they want everyone to be healthy and not be seduced into immorality by provocative or outrageous clothing. The truth is, they just like to be in control.

Fur and fowl

Obesity was clearly a major problem in medieval times. In 1336, Edward III passed the Sumptuary Act which prohibited any man to have more than two courses at a meal. It even sought to restrain those who pretended that soup was actually a sauce so that it did not count as a course in its own right. On feast days, though, three courses were permitted.

In fact, Edward III passed so many laws about food and dress that in 1363 he consolidated them all in the Statute of Diet and Apparel. This warned ploughmen particularly to eat moderately, but also enjoined lords to give their servants fish or fresh meat once a day, along with any leftover milk, butter and cheese.

Laws to curb excessive eating and drink were also enacted by Edward IV and, of all people, Henry VIII. His sickly son Edward VI repealed them all but, to help the fishing industry, he passed a law banning the eating of meat on Fridays and Saturdays, and during Lent, except for the sick.

By the reign of Elizabeth I, the penalty for eating meat when prohibited was £3 or three months' imprisonment. But not eating meat on certain days of the week was not a religious duty, as some Catholics maintain today. Elizabeth had no time for popery and condemned anyone who preached that not eating meat helped 'save your soul or was a service to God' to be punished as a 'spreader of false news'.

James I abolished the exemption for the sickly, and justices of the peace were authorised to enter victualling houses and impound meat found there. England's dietary laws were only repealed by Queen Victoria, who grew rather stout herself.

Adulteration of tea

Under the Adulteration of Tea Act of 1776, anyone found in possession of more than six pounds of 'sloe leaves, or the leaves of ash, elder or any other tree' was required to prove that they had gathered them with the consent of the owners of the tree. They also had to prove that the leaves were gathered for a use other than 'the purpose of fabricating and manufacturing the same in imitation of tea'. If they could not, the fine was £5, or between six months and a year in gaol. The earlier 1730 Adulteration of Tea Act also sets the penalty for 'sophisticating tea' at £10.

What not to wear

In 1337, Edward III passed a law banning anyone including the King, Queen, their children, prelates, earls, barons, knight, ladies and men of the Church from wearing fur.

With Edward's Labourers and Artificers Act of 1350, he aimed to curb 'the malice of servants, which were idle, and not willing to serve after the pestilence' – that is, the Black Death, which hit England in 1349 killing up to half the population. This resulted in a shortage of labour. Surviving peasants demanded 'excessive wages', which this statute was enacted to prevent. It also specified that 'Shoes &c shall be sold as in the 20th year of King Edward III'. In other words, peasants were not to adopt the fashions of the nobility, but rather content themselves with the peasant dress they wore before the plague arrived.

In the 1363 Statute of Diet and Apparel, Edward III detailed the proper attire for each class to wear, at the same time fixing the price they were to pay. Craftsmen, for example, were not to wear clothes worth more than 40 shillings – £2 – and their families were not to wear silk, fur or silk velvet.

Ploughmen were to wear a blanket with a linen girdle – simple but functional. No female member of a servant's family was to wear a girdle trimmed with silver. Every person beneath the rank of a lord was to wear a jacket that reached his knees, and only lords were allowed to wear shoes with points more than two inches long.

Only the royal family could wear gold cloth or purple silk and no one below the rank of knight could wear velvet, damask, satin, foreign wool or sable. On the other hand, the King could issue special licences allowing the bearer to wear whatever he authorised.

The penalties were harsh for wearing unauthorised garments. Anyone with an annual income below £20 who had the audacity to wear a silk nightcap got three months in jail, or a fine of £10 for each night.

During the reign of Henry VIII, a law was passed limiting the width of shoes to six inches. And to encourage the wool trade, Elizabeth I passed a law saying that anyone over the age of six who was not a 'lady or a gentleman' had to wear 'a cap of wool knit and dressed in England' on the Sabbath. She also made the penalty for taking live sheep out of the country forfeiture of goods and imprisonment for a year. At the end of that year, the prisoner's left hand was to be cut off in a market square and nailed up in a public place. The export of wool was one of the first offences to attract the penalty of transportation.

Under Charles II, again to help the wool trade, a law was passed requiring coffins to be lined with fleece and shrouds to be made of wool.

Make-up

Elizabeth I passed a law that aimed to ban any woman leading a man into marriage through the use of false hair, make-up, false hips, high-heeled shoes or other such devices. She was to be punished with the penalties as witchcraft.

CHAPTER SEVEN

Courtroom Capers

HE LAW IS SUPPOSED to be a solemn and dignified process – people's lives and liberties depend upon it – but sometimes the strange goings-on in English courtrooms defy all logic.

Arresting juries

Jury duty used to be a much more onerous task than it is today – in Elizabethan times it was not uncommon for jurors to be fined or imprisoned if they disagreed with the judge. In the reign of James I the Lord Chancellor, the two chief justices and the Chief Baron got together and decided that when the accused was found guilty in the indictment then the decision of the jury should not be questioned; but when a jury acquitted a prisoner against what the court held to be proof of guilt, they should charged in the court of the Star Chamber 'for their partiality in finding a manifest offender not guilty'.

In 1667, Chief Justice Kelynge extended this to grand juries, ignoring their decisions on the grounds that they had not considered them sufficiently. He fined a grand jury in Somerset for not finding against a man accused of murder, though the report says that 'because they were gentlemen of repute in the county, the court spared the fine.' He made a habit of fining and imprisoning juries who refused to convict dissenters, but he went too far when he dismissed one offender's appeal to Magna Carta, echoing Cromwell with the words: 'Magna Carta – Magna Farta.' He was hauled before of the House of Commons, which then ruled that 'the precedents and practice of fining or imprisoning jurors for verdicts is illegal'.

The change in the law had come about not because of an Act of Parliament but because of the courage of a jury. On 14 August 1670 William Penn and his fellow Quaker, William Meade, found that their meeting house in Grace Church Street had been padlocked by the authorities, so they addressed a crowd of several hundred in the street outside in direct contravention of the Conventicle Act of 1664, which was designed to suppress non-conformist religions and specifically forbade ministers preaching to their congregations in the open air. But Penn and Meade were not just charged under the Conventicle Act; the authorities also pressed the more serious charge of 'unlawfully and tumultuously' calling and addressing an assembly 'to the terror and disturbance of His Majesty's subjects' – a capital offence.

The two men appeared in the Old Bailey on 1 September 1670 and the trial dragged on for five days, at the end of which the jury found Penn and Meade not guilty. But the verdict of 12 good men and true was not good enough for the judge.

'I will have a positive verdict or you'll starve for it,' he bellowed, and the jury were locked up for two days without food or water, heat or light.

Led by Edward Bushell and Thomas Vere, they refused to give way, so the judge fined the jurymen 40 marks. They refused to pay and the judge sent them to prison until they did so. Eventually they were released when the Lord Chief Justice, Sir John Vaughan, intervened, conceding to the principle that a judge 'may try to open the eyes of the jurors, but not to lead them by the nose'. Plainly if the jury were to find as the judge instructed there would be no point in trial by jury.

When Bushell was released, he took out a writ to free Penn and Meade, for although the original 'not guilty' verdict stood, they had subsequently been fined and gaoled for not removing their hats in court.

The trial, which is known as 'Bushell's Case', stands as a landmark in legal history, having established beyond question the independence of the jury. On the wall of the Central Criminal Court – the Old Bailey – there is a plaque paying tribute to the 'courage and endurance' of Bushell, Vere and the rest of the jurymen.

Carting the jury

It has long been the practice for judges to travel in a circuit around the provinces, judging cases at assizes in various county towns along the way. But what happens if the jury has yet to reach a decision in a case when the time comes for the judge to move on? The solution was laid down in a case in 1670: 'If the jury cannot agree before the judges depart, they are to be carried in carts after them, so they may give their verdict out of the county.'

Shop until you drop

Until the reign of Edward III, all the courts used to follow the King as he travelled around the country. Indeed, a law passed by Edward I in 1309 insisted that the Lord Chancellor and King's Bench follow him where he went, so if you wanted to get a judgement in a case you were constantly on the move. But with the beginnings of the Hundred Years' War, Edward III wanted to spend more time in France, so the King's Bench and the Chancery settled in Westminster Hall. The two courts sat in the open hall – which must have caused some confusion – with the King's Bench occupying the left-hand side of the room and the Chancery the right-hand side, with a bar to keep the crowd back to prevent them swamping the judge. The Chancellor, 'on account of his superior dignity', sat on a marble chair on a raised platform.

To add to the confusion, there were also shops in the Hall which did brisk business during the hearings and continued doing so until 1630 when, one Saturday night, a woman left a pan of hot coals under a stall and the shops caught fire. The Hall itself was only saved when two sailors climbed up on the roof, opened the lead and poured water down on the flames. After that Charles I ordered that there should be no more shopping done in his courtrooms.

CHAPTER EIGHT

Other Jurisdictions

 N SOME RESPECTS THE United Kingdom is not that united. Although English law has spread its writ around the world, there are many parts of the homeland where different rules apply.

The Channel Islands

The Channel Islands are dependencies of the English Crown and not strictly part of the UK. They were part of the Duchy of Normandy and their laws are mostly ducal customs laid out in an ancient thirteenth-century Norman book known as *Le Grand Coustumier*. These laws were revised in the reign of Elizabeth I and became the island's legal code. To this day, Acts of the British Parliament do not apply in the islands unless they specifically say so and cases there are tried in the islands' own courts.

The islands are divided into two bailiwicks – Guernsey and Jersey – each with its own constitution. Although Alderney, Sark, Herm, Brecqhou, Jethou and Lihou are part of

Guernsey's bailiwick, and Les Minquiers and the Ecrehous rocks are part of Jersey's, the smaller inhabited islands have laws of their own.

The rights and custom of the two 'states' are medieval in origin. The *Bailli* – bailiff or chief magistrate – is the first law officer of each island, and he traditionally retains his office for life and presides at the Royal Court. He used to take the opinion of the elected Jucats, but retains the casting vote in both civil and criminal cases. Trial by jury was introduced in 1786. Unlike the English system of 12 jurors, island juries had 24 members – if 20 agreed on a guilty verdict, the accused was convicted; if not, they were freed.

The *Bailli* is appointed by the Crown and is not required to have any legal training, though they have usually held some position in the island bar. Until 1860, only six advocates were allowed to practise in the court of Jersey, and they were nominated by the *Bailli*. After that, the bar was thrown open to any British subject who had been resident on the island for ten years, was a member of the English bar, had taken a law degree at a French university and had passed the local bar examination.

In Jersey there were punitive laws concerning debt which an unwary Englishman fell foul of in 1861. If you did not pay a bill presented by a landowner – no matter how outrageously inflated – you were thrown in gaol until the matter was settled. While in custody you had to pay for your upkeep, plus ten shillings – 50p – for the gaoler to open the prison door to let you attend court. If the court found against you, you had to pay the whole amount, including the gaol fees, before you were discharged. Yet if the court found in your favour, there was no redress for the time you spent in gaol.

Jurats who sat on a case could also hear the appeal and, to make things worse for visiting Englismen, the proceedings were heard in French.

Making a *Clameur*

In the Channel Islands, it is possible to obtain an ad hoc injunction by means of the *Clameur de Haro*, which is a call for aid to Rollo, the first Duke of Normandy, who died in AD 932. To do this, you must go down on one knee with your head bared within earshot of two witnesses and cry: '*Haro, haro, haro, à l'aide, mon prince: on me fait tort.*' (Hear-ye, hear-ye, hear-ye, come to my aid, my lord: I am being wronged.) Then recite the Lord's Prayer in French.

Originally this had also had to be done within earshot of the defendant, but the courts ruled that the cry can be raised in absentia – particularly if the defendant is out of the country. This is important as the *clameur* can be raised against the authorities whose leader, the English monarch, it unlikely to be at hand. Even if the offender is on the island they cannot run off out of earshot. Once the words '*haro, haro, haro*' have been said, the offender is deemed to have heard the *clameur*.

Originally, the *clameur* had to be raised between sunrise and sunset, but that dated from a time when it was an ecclesiastical offence to work before sunrise and after sunset. These days raising the *clameur* is a 24-hour right, although it can only be raised in the face of an *appert péril* – an immediate danger – and '*pour conserver et non pour recouvrer*' – to conserve but not recover – rights inherent in land, the inheritance of 'real property' or its 'quiet enjoyment'. It can be raised when the ownership of property is in dispute, but only when the one who raises it has been in possession of the property and believes 'in good faith' that they own it.

In Sark, there is a variation. The criant must bare his head and before witnesses cry out: '*Haro, haro, haro! Au nom de Dieu et de la Reine, laissez ce travail.*' Failure to bare the head in Sark invalidates the clameur, the idea of baring the head being that the witnesses can clearly recognise the *criant*.

The *clameur* originated as a means of summoning neighbours and passers-by to aid the victim of a crime and there were penalties for failure to respond to the *criant*'s aid or join in the pursuit, just as there were for raising the cry falsely.

Sark

Of all the Channel Islands Sark is strangest, being the last feudal state in Europe and boasting numerous strange laws. Its constitution dates from Letters Patent given by Elizabeth I to Helier de Carteret in 1565, which allowed him to maintain the old Norman feudal laws and cost him £50 for the privilege. In exchange he had to hold the island against the pirates who plagued shipping in the Channel at that time and to do so he was obliged to keep a force of 40 men on the island at all times.

As Seigneurs of Sark, Helier and his heirs were not allowed give away or sell any land in the Fief of Sark without royal permission, so to fulfil his defence obligation, he sold off 40 perpetual tenures to his defence force. Under feudal laws these tenements were passed on intact by primogeniture, that is, the oldest son inherited the whole parcel of land. In recent times, to comply with European Human Rights legislation the tenure can be handed on to either a son or a daughter, and not necessarily the oldest one – although the land still cannot be divided. Consequently, divorce is not allowed on the island, and in theory, each tenement must supply a man with a musket for the defence of the island.

There are a few sub-tenancies because early on some land divided in defiance of the law, although this was stopped by new Letters Patent issued in 1611 by James I. More recently, special permission had to be sought from Her Majesty's Procurer to alienate land to build the lighthouse, the telephone exchange and the medical centre.

The 40 tenants paid for their tenements by tithes, whereby when crops were harvested, every tenth sheaf was loaded onto the Seigneur's tithe cart. The tithe also applied to lands, wool, cider and minerals, but these rights are currently suspended. The 40 tenants also sat as the island's parliament, the Chief Pleas, to speak on behalf the people of their tenement, but deputies are now elected to advise the Seigneur.

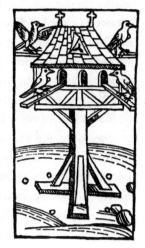

Despite this concession to democracy, the Seigneur retains certain feudal rights. The Seigneur – who is currently a Dame – is the only one allowed to keep a bitch, a feudal custom that was one way for the Seigneur to preserved their hunting rights. The Seigneur also maintains the *droit du columbier* – the right to keep a dovecot. However, even this right has been diluted as in recent years the Dame has allowed one resident of Sark to keep a flock of racing pigeons.

Until the end of the eighteenth century, the Seigneur also had the sole right to mill flour, but in 1797 the islanders set fire to the windmill built by Helier de Carteret as a protest against the Seigneur's monopoly. The Royal Court in Guernsey upheld the right of one Thomas de Carteret to mill flour in his own windmill and a second unofficial windmill was built on the peninsula of Little Sark. Today the Dame mills the island's flour using modern machinery.

One law that is strictly enforced is the ban on importing cars. Tractors are allowed, but their use is strictly regulated, the current Dame maintaining that there should be one spot left on Earth undisturbed by modern means of transport.

Isle of Man

Legally the Isle of Man is not part of the English realm – it belonged to the Norwegian Crown until 1266, when it was sold to Scotland; then in 1341, the English Crown seized it and granted it as a fiefdom to Sir John Stanley, whose heirs held the island until 1736 when the Dukes of Atholl took over. But the British Parliament purchased its sovereignty in 1765 and bought the rest of the Atholl family's prerogatives on the island in 1828.

Until 1417, the Manx laws were said to be 'locked up in the breasts of the Deemsters' – two judges who each had jurisdiction in the north and south of the island. Sir John Stanley suspected that the Deemsters were just making the laws up as they went along and ordered a promulgation, forcing them to proclaim them, but it did no good. The 'breast laws' continued for another two centuries until 1636 when the Deemsters were finally forced to 'set down in writing, and certify what these breast laws are'. Despite this, as judges, the Deemsters were seen to be impartial as they were bound by a curious oath, which said: 'I do swear that I will execute the laws of the isle justly betwixt party and party as indifferently as the herring's backbone doth lie in the midst of the fish.'

In 1777 and 1813, Manx laws were amended in an attempt to simplify them, but each defendant was still allowed three separate and distinct trials before different bodies. First the High Bailiff would hear the case; then it would be considered by a Deemster and six jurymen; and finally it would be tried by the Governor and the Deemsters. By that time the charges would have been paired down, so the defendant would be tried on the most lenient statute possible. The only people the Manx courts were hard on were debtors and if it was suspected someone was going to leave the island without paying their debts, they would be locked up in Castle Rushden.

As well the High Bailiff's court and the two Deemsters' courts, the island also boasted courts of Chancery, Admiralty, General Gaol Delivery, Exchequer and Common Law, along with a Seneschal's court, a Consistorial court and a Licensing court. Each subdivision, or sheading, had its own coroner or sheriff, who could appoint a 'lockman' or gaoler as his deputy. And each of the seventeen parishes had its own captain and 'sumner', whose duty was to keep order in church and 'beat all the doggs'.

Until 1866, the House of Keys – the elected chamber of the Isle of Man's parliament or Tynwald – had a judicial as well as a legislative function. Since Norse times, it joined with the

Legislative Council, the upper house, to form the Tynwald Court which assembled every 5 July – Tynwald Day – to read out the new laws. According to Sir Hall Caine, who witnessed the event in the late nineteenth century: 'The proceedings were, in themselves, long, tiresome, ineffectual, formless, unimpressive and unpicturesque … Hardly anybody heard them; hardly anybody listened.'

The laws of Man

Law on the Isle of Man was also administered by the ecclesiastical court and the bishop had his own prison, a dungeon in the crypt of St German's Cathedral, which is incorporated into Peel Castle. Most of the crime prosecuted by the ecclesiastical court on the Isle of Man – with the exception of illegal salmon fishing – seems to have involved fornication.

In 1705, William Kissack was found guilty of committing adultery and incest with the daughter of his wife's sister. After a month's incarceration in the bishop's dungeon he was sentenced to perform penance at each of the island's parish churches, wearing nothing but a white sheet and carrying a white wand with a list of his crimes pinned to his chest.

Women received even harsher punishment. The traditional penalty for sexual immorality was to be dragged behind a boat across one of the island's harbours. Katherine Kindred was sentenced to be 'dragged after a boat at Peeltown' on 17 March 1714 for being 'a notorious strumpet, who has brought forth three illegitimate children, and still continues to stroll about the country, and to lead a most vicious and scandalous life on other accounts'.

Sexual slander was also common. In 1678, Margaret Huiston of Braddan was put in the stocks for one hour at the height of the market in Douglas for saying that Catherine Christian was a whore who 'got pieces of fustian from Scotchmen for lying with her'. She also had to beg forgiveness from Catherine on her knees and make penance for two Sundays – all of which was to be followed by 40 days imprisonment. She got off lightly as the usual punishment for defamation well into the eighteenth century was to be put in the island's version of the scold's bridle. According to a visitor in 1726, those convicted were sentenced 'to stand in the market-place in a sort of scaffold erected for the purpose with their tongue in a noose made of leather, which they call the bridle, and having thus been exposed to the view of the people for some time, on the taking off this machine they were obliged to say three times: "Tongue, thou hast lyed."'

Wales

Wales only became subject to English law during the reign of Henry VIII, when it was administered by a high constable appointed for each hundred. Once appointed the candidate had to serve, or answer to, the justices. It was an unpaid position and during the sixteenth, seventeenth and eighteenth centuries it was commonly held that no greater calamity could befall a man than to be appointed high constable. Duties included collecting the rates, attending court and ordering vagrants to be whipped. In 1831, one high constable calculated that the office cost him £30 out of his own pocket. The office was only abolished in 1856 when the Counties and Boroughs Police Act established new county constabularies.

Begging bards

After the rebellion of Owen Glendower in 1400–09, Henry IV passed a series of Penal Laws which prevented Welsh people from owning land or holding office in any town in Wales or the Marches. They could not carry weapons, fortify their houses, meet in large gatherings without permission, be members of juries or give guilty verdicts against English people. If an Englishman married a Welsh woman, he would lose his own rights. These laws were still in force in 1536 when the Act of Union was passed.

The fifteenth-century decree also stated: 'No rimers, minstrels or vagabonds [should] be maintained in Wales whom by their divination, lies and exhortations are partly cause for insurrection and rebellion now in Wales.'

When Elizabeth I came to the throne, she was determined to clamp down on vagrancy, but in Wales bards had traditionally survived by begging. So in her 1568 proclamation banning vagrancy, Elizabeth set up the Eisteddfod, so that true bards could be distinguished from idle beggars.

Scotland

In Scotland, particularly, there were strict laws concerning sexual behaviour, which were often administered by the Church. Gossip, slander, adultery and fornication appear frequently in the records of Kirk sessions. For a first offence, the guilty party would be required to stand on a stool or 'pillar' of penitence, dressed in sackcloth, outside the church on Sunday, sometimes outside every church in the Presbytery.

Some men could not stand the humiliation. In 1574, Robert Drummond slit his throat on being accused of adultery; a cobbler in Edinburgh went mad in 1693 when ordered to provide a sackcloth gown that he was going to be publicly exhibited in; and in 1736 George Porteous hanged himself rather than face the ordeal.

There were also more general fines for fornication, known charmingly as 'buttock-mail'. For the first offence, the fine was four Scottish pounds – which was eight shillings (40p) sterling, which was doubled for a second offence. Adultery incurred a fine of £20 (Scottish), with £40 for a second offence.

For repeated offences jougs were used. This was a heavy iron collar attached to the church wall by a chain at a height of about five feet. The weight alone caused great discomfort and if the offender's knees gave way they risked strangulation.

In the seventeenth century, the minister at Tyningham wrote that he 'regretted that their were troublemakers in the town, especially women, and that they troubled the session so often, and he earnestly desired that the civil magistrate concur in punishing them, and that jougs might be made at the kirk door, wherein delinquents might be put'.

The last time the jougs at the Mercat Cross outside Haddington were used was in 1785 when a servant of the distiller David Gourlay stole some brandy. He was put on the jougs for an hour on 30 September with a sign around his neck saying he was an 'infamous thief of his master's property'.

In Tranent, they had a more informal system of punishment – a man who made advances to his neighbour's wife was visited by a mob at night, who tied him to the back of a pony in his nightshirt and paraded him around town. For a similar offence, a woman would be made to 'ride the strang' – she would be made to sit astride a pole that was raised to shoulder height, and after she had been carried around town to the jeers of the mob, she would be dumped unceremoniously in the loch.

'Promiscuous dancing' – that is, men and women dancing together – was also against the law and a bridegroom would often have to stump up a large surety against promiscuous dancing taking place at his wedding reception.

It was against the law for women to sit in church with their plaids covering their heads, as the Church elders could not see whether they were asleep or not – if found guilty, they would be tarred. In 1643, the Kirk sessions of Monifieth provided their officer Robert Scott 'with ane pynt of tar' for the purpose.

CHAPTER NINE

Curious Cases

ESPITE THE BULGING statute books, the architects of our laws could not think of every eventuality and judges have to adjudicate as necessary. As there are numerous scenarios that our lawmakers never envisaged, the ingenuity of judges is constantly being put to the test by curious cases – which themselves make law. Every new decision made by an English judge becomes woven into the fabric of the law – and not just in this country. Rulings made in English courts are cited in courts through common-law countries, including India and the United States.

Responsibility for animals

The law can never quite make up its mind who is responsible for the actions of animals. Whereas on the Continent there are many incidents of malfeasant animals appearing in the dock, this does not occur in Britain – although the owner of the animal in question is sometimes held responsible, the law is not very consistent on the subject.

In a case in 1943, a lawyer had cause to bewail the fact that 'a farmer who allows his cow to stray through a gap in his hedge on to his neighbour's land, where it consumes a few cauliflowers, is liable in damages to his neighbour, but if, through a similar gap in the hedge, it strays on to the road and causes the overturning of a motor omnibus, with the death or injury of thirty or forty people, he is under no liability at all.'

This question took an even more bizarre turn in Inverness in 1954, when a cow broke free from the auction at a cattle market, escaped through an unsecured gate into the street, climbed some stairs and fell through the upper floor into the shop below, where, in its struggles, it turned on a tap and flooded the place.

The shopkeeper sued the auctioneer's firm for damages, but the judge said that he found himself 'forced to the conclusion that a gate-crashing, stair-climbing, floor-bursting, tap-turning cow was something *sui generis*' – a unique case – 'for whose depredations the law affords no remedy unless there was foreknowledge of some such propensities'.

Cattle levant and couchant

The laws controlling the grazing of animals on common land go back to feudal times, but cause dissent to this day. A Mr Estler owned a 5½-acre smallholding in Effingham in Surrey which he farmed with the aid of his 19-year-old horse William. In the summer, he would graze the horse on the common, but the local lord of the manor, Mr Murells, took exception, claiming that Estler had no right to graze the horse on common land and impounding William.

Estler sued on the grounds that the 5½ acres of land he owned entitled him to grazing rights, but the suit failed when the medieval principle of 'levancy and couchancy' was envoked. Under that principle only the number of animals that could be supported on the owner's own land, 'levant and couchant' – standing and lying, as the law picturesquely puts it – in winter can be grazed on common land in the summer. Much of Mr Estler's land was arable and there were only two acres for William to be levant and couchant on during the winter months, and a horse needs around a ton of hay to get it through the winter – more than could be produced by two acres. So Estler lost and had to compensate Mr Murells for the common-land grass William had already eaten.

Plaintiff, judge and jury

It makes it much easier to decide a case if the plaintiff is also the judge and selects the jury – as was the case in the reign of Henry VIII, when a quarrel broke out among the Berkeley family. As part of the feud a number of Maurice Berkeley's servants entered the park of Lady Anne Berkeley at Yate in Gloucestershire, killed the deer and set fire to the haystacks. When she complained to the King, he issued a special commission, authorising her to inquire into the cause of the trouble. She returned to Gloucester, 'opened the commission, sat on the bench, empanelled a jury, and heard the charge, and on a verdict of guilty pronounced sentence accordingly', says a report of the trial.

Sent to Coventry

The Maiming Act of 1670 was passed after Sir John Coventry was attacked in the streets by a number of armed men, some of whom held him down while others slit his nose. It was thought the motive was revenge. Also known as the Coventry Act, the 1670 law made it a felony to lie in wait, with malice aforethought, and 'unlawfully cut out or disable a tongue, put out an eye, slit a nose, cut off a nose or a lip or disable any limb … with intend to maim or disfigure'. The punishment: death without benefit of clergy.

The Act was not repealed until 1828 and came in handy in a curious case in 1772. A man named Coke hired a labourer named Woodburn to kill his brother-in-law, a gentleman named Crispe. Woodburn attacked Crispe with a billhook used for trimming hedges and left him for dead, but Crispe survived and recovered, though he was terribly disfigured.

The trouble was that attempted murder was not a felony, so charges were laid under the Coventry Act – against Woodburn for the actual offence, and against Coke for hiring and abetting him. Coke protested in court that the intent was to murder Crispe, not to disfigure him, therefore, he contended, he was not guilty under the statute for which he had been indicted. But the court held that if a man attacked another with a billhook, there was automatically a danger that the victim would be disfigured. The jury found the prisoners guilty and they were condemned and executed.

Dishonour among thieves

Some things are better settled out of court. In 1725, there was a disagreement between two highwaymen, who took the matter to law. The plaintiff, a man named Everet, claimed that he was 'skilled in dealing in several sorts of commodities' – particularly rings, watches, precious metals and the like. He claimed that the defendant, Williams, had asked to become his partner and they agreed verbally to go into business together, which included splitting the costs of horses, saddles, bridles and all the other necessities of their profession. Equally, all their expenses on the road and in taverns, inns, alehouses, markets and fairs would be divided equally between them.

Once that was settled, they 'proceeded jointly in the said dealings with good success on Hounslow Heath, where they dealt with a gentleman for a gold watch'. Then they proceeded to Finchley in Middlesex which, the plaintiff said, 'was a good and convenient place to deal in, and that commodities were very plenty'. Their dealings there were 'almost all gain to them' and they 'dealt with several gentlemen for divers watches, rings, swords, canes, hats, cloaks, horses, bridles, saddles and other things to the value of £200 and upwards'.

After about a month, they moved on to Blackheath, where Williams had heard that there was a gentleman who had a good horse, saddle, bridle, watch, sword, cane and other things to dispose of which 'might be had for little or no money, in case they could prevail on the said gentleman to part with the said things'. Everet said that, indeed, 'after some small discourse with the said gentleman' he agreed to part with them 'at a very cheap rate'.

Everet and Williams continued about their business in Bagshot, Salisbury, Hampstead and other places, accumulating over £2,000, but when they parted at Michaelmas, Everet maintained that Williams 'would not come to a fair account touching and concerning the said partnership'.

The judge took a dim view of this. He fined the plaintiff's two solicitors for contempt, and counsel was ordered to pay costs. The defendant was hanged at Maidstone in 1727, and the plaintiff at Tyburn in 1730; later, in 1735, one of the plaintiff's solicitors was convicted of robbery and transported.

Malicious prosecution

In 1639, a man named Pigot indicted his stepmother for poisoning her husband, his father. She was acquitted and brought an action against him for malicious prosecution, which she won, recovering substantial damages. However, when her stepson appealed, the case was heard at the King's Bench where, this time, she was convicted, taken back to Berkshire, where the offence had occurred, and burned.

The king over the water

In Hereford in 1944, a defendant who held on to property that belonged to someone else under the provisions of a will, claimed that the Court of Probate Act of 1857 was not law because it had not received royal assent. The Act had been signed by Queen Victoria, but the defendant claimed that the true royal succession was with the Stuart line, which laid himself open to prosecution for treason, or at the very least praemunire. Under English law, this is the crime of asserting papal supremacy in England, a crime committed by claiming the Catholic descendants of James II are the true kings of England. The punishment involves life imprisonment and forfeiture of all property to the Crown. It also puts the offender outside the protection of the Crown, so he cannot bring or defend an action. As it was, the court simply ruled against him.

Christ, a bad precedent

In 1794, an Englishman named Gerald was tried for sedition before Lord Justice Clerk Braxfield in Edinburgh. Although a number of able counsels offered their services, the accused decided to defend himself, believing he was one of the most eloquent speakers of his time. However, he was no lawyer and forgot that the law was governed by precedent. Claiming that he was not a revolutionary, he said, 'It was reform, not revolution, for which I have striven, and Jesus Christ was himself a reformer.'

But Lord Braxfield immediately spotted that a precedent had been cited. 'Well, sir, much did he get by that,' said the judge. 'Wasn't he crucified?'

Slow justice

The longest lawsuit before the English courts was between the heirs of Sir Thomas Talbot and the heirs of Lord Barkly, and concerned land in Gloucestershire, near Wotton-under-Edge. The suit began in the reign of Edward IV (1461–1483) and ended at the beginning of the reign of James I (1603–1625).

Rough justice

In 1749, Mr Justice Willes tried a young man named Paul Wells for forgery at the Oxford assizes. The offence was a trivial one – he had altered the date on a bond, so that he would not have to pay it until the following year. Although technically it was a capital offence, the judge assured him of a pardon when the judgement was sent to the King with his recommendation. But Judge Willes was a friend of the Prince of Wales who the King loathed – and against all precedent George II rejected the judge's recommendation for a pardon and Wells was hanged.

A special appeal

In 1722, a highwayman named Hartley was convicted of stealing the clothes of a journeyman tailor, leaving him tied naked to a tree. Although there was no doubt as to his guilt, a special appeal was made on his behalf. Six attractive young women, dressed in white, went to St James's Palace to present a petition on his behalf, their appearance alone guaranteeing their admittance. They told the King that if he pardoned the highwayman, they would draw lots to see who would be Hartley's wife. But George I was not moved, telling them that the prisoner was more deserving of the gallows than a wife – and he was hanged.

Against the law to murder a ghost

In 1804, when Hammersmith was still a quiet village near London, a ghost was seen there. It was such a ghastly apparition that it scared a heavily pregnant woman to death – at least, she died two days after seeing it. Later a waggoner ran for his life when he saw it, leaving behind a team of eight horses and sixteen passengers.

But Francis Smith was made of sterner stuff. When he saw the ghost on the streets of Hammersmith one night, he pulled out a gun and shot it – only to find that the apparition was in fact a miller returning home late from work, covered in flour. A jury found him guilty of manslaughter, but the judge sent them back, instructing them that they must either acquit him or find him guilty of murder. They convicted him on a charge of murder and the judge sentenced him to death, although the sentence was later commuted to one year's imprisonment.

The slave trade

The Atlantic slave trade was abolished in the courtrooms of England long before Parliament addressed the problem. As early as 1579, it was judged that 'the air of England was too pure for a slave to breathe in', and in 1749 a court established that 'there is no such thing as a slave by the law of England'. In 1762, a judge ruled that 'as soon as a man sets foot on English ground he is free: a negro may maintain an action against his master for ill usage, and may have a *habeas corpus* if restrained of his liberty'.

Ten years later a writ of habeas corpus was issued in the case of a black man named James Sommersett, who was 'confined in irons on board a ship called *Ann and Mary*, John Knowles commander, lying in the Thames, and bound for Jamaica'. Hearing the case, Lord Mansfield judged that although Sommersett had not set foot on English soil, he was breathing English air and ordered him to be set free.

Mansfield made another landmark ruling in the abolition of the slave trade. It concerned a British ship named *Zong* which left the coast of Guinea on 6 September 1781 bound for Jamaica, carrying a cargo of 440 slaves and a crew of 17. By the time she reached the Caribbean, the complement was down to 380 slaves and 10 crewmen, many of whom were sick.

The *Zong* approached Jamaica on 27 November, but her captain, Luke Collingwood, steered away, saying that he mistook the island for another one. Two days later, he called the remains of his crew together and revealed his murderous plan – he proposed throwing overboard all the sick slaves. They were unlikely to recover, he said, and they would fetch nothing at auction. His justification was that the ship was short of water and, by throwing some of the slaves overboard, he would be able to save the rest.

The real reason was an insurance swindle. Insurers would not pay out for a slave who died of natural causes, fearing that the slavers would simply let the slaves die. But the rule of the sea is that an insurer has to pay up for cargo thrown overboard if the reason for jettisoning it is to save the rest, and although this rule was not written with a human cargo in mind, it still applied.

The mate, James Kelsal, objected, saying that as they were not short of water and were near land there was no justification for throwing anyone overboard. However, having made his protest, Kelsal said no more and indeed was one of the men who threw 54 slaves alive into the sea, where they drowned. Three days later, after rain had replenished their stocks of water, 42 more were thrown overboard, and a week later, as they neared land, a further 26. To prevent them swimming ashore, their arms were bound before they were thrown overboard. Another ten jumped overboard of their own accord.

A few days later, the *Zong* anchored in the harbour in Kingston, Jamaica, where the rest of the slaves were sold. Collingwood duly put in a claim for the 122 men and women he and his men had drowned and the ten who had killed themselves. However, the insurers were suspicious, investigated the claim and found out what had happened.

When the insurers refused to pay up for the drowned slaves they were sued by the owners, who won the case by arguing that throwing 132 slaves overboard was no different, in law, to throwing 132 horses overboard. The insurers appealed, whereupon Lord Mansfield reversed the decision on the grounds that human beings – slaves included – could not be treated simply as goods.

The case brought about the campaign for the abolition of the slave trade and there were even calls to charge the *Zong's* officers with murder, but in the meantime Collingwood had died and nothing came of it. William Wilberforce started the Society for Effecting the Abolition of the Slave Trade in 1787 and his bill to abolish the slave trade in the British West Indies was passed in 1807.

CHAPTER TEN

The Word is Law

HE LAW IS ALL ABOUT WORDS, whether written down in the statute books or spoken in court, and it is wise to use them carefully.

Language of the law

In 1362, the Chancellor, William de Edington, carried through Parliament a statute requiring that all future pleadings and judgements before the courts should be made in English. Since the Norman Conquest, all court proceedings had been in French.

But de Edington's law took a little time to catch on in practice. It was only when Richard III – Shakespeare's villain – seized power in 1483 that he began writing laws in English, although lawyers reverted to Latin. The Commonwealth again insisted that the language of the law was English, but during the Restoration law reports again appeared in French, whereas law records were kept in barbarous – that is, not classical – Latin. This continued until the mid-eighteenth century and was only changed under George II, who was more comfortable speaking German. Nevertheless law reports continued to use '*chemin*' instead of 'road', '*dismes*' instead of 'tithes' and '*baron* and *feme*' instead of 'husband and wife'.

In Parliament Norman French is still used today several centuries later. Royal assent is given to a bill with the words '*La Reyne le veult.*' The House of Lords endorses a bill with the words '*A ceste Bille les Seigneurs sont assentus.*' When a bill fails, it lists the reasons that it does not agree with the House of Commons under the heading '*Ceste Bille est remise aux Seigneurs avecque des raison.*' And, by tradition, at the beginning of each parliament, the Lords make an entry in their journals, in French, of the appointment of receivers and triers of petitions, not only for England, but also for Gascony.

English, by tradition, is also the language of the law in America – or at least most of it. In 1919, the legendary journalist and author H.L. Mencken successfully lobbied to have an Illinois statute revised, establishing 'American' as the official language of the state.

Do they mean 'not'?

The Justices of the Peace Act of 1361, which is still in force, is missing a vital word, 'not'. The Act gives those selected to be justices the power to bind over to be of good behaviour '*touz ceux qi sont de bone fame*' – which means 'all them that be of good fame [or reputation]'. Plainly there is a 'ne' missing somewhere. To this day, the matter has not been resolved.

Catch-all titles

In 1536, Henry VIII signed an all-encompassing statute entitled: An Act for the Continue of the Statutes for Beggars and Vagabonds; and against Conveyance of Horses and Mares out of this Realm; against Welshmen making Affrays in the Counties of Hereford, Gloucester and Salop; and against the vice of Buggery. Are these offences in some way connected?

Short and sweet

While most statutes are long winded, the shortest seems to be one from 1483, which reads: 'None from henceforth shall use to multiply gold or silver, or use the craft of multiplications, and if any do the same, he shall incur the pain of felony.' It seems to be warning you not to get rich quick and comes immediately before another, more straightforward, felony – that incurred by cutting the tongue or plucking out the eyes of the King's liege men.

Swift passage

The process of passing a bill through Parliament is usually protracted, but in 1779 one was passed in just three days. At twenty past twelve one night, as the House of Commons was about to adjourn, Attorney-General Wedderburn rose and, without any previous notice, moved 'for leave to bring in a bill to suspend all exemptions from impressment into the navy, together with the right of those impressed to sue with a writ of *habeas corpus* for their liberation'.

Although this gave the government the power to conscript the entire population of Great Britain, the bill was introduced at one o'clock and read a first and second time. The following day it was sent to the Lords, and on the third day it receive royal assent.

Nuts

When the British government set up the loss-making ground-nut scheme in Africa in 1947, a law was passed which contained a paragraph that read: 'In the Nuts (unground) (other than ground-nuts) Order, the expression nuts shall have reference to such nuts, other than ground-nuts, as would but for this amending Order not qualify as nuts (unground) (other than ground-nuts) by reason of their being nuts (unground).'

False start

Under the Customs Consolidation Act of 1876 it is impossible to sue a customs officer. Section 268 says that no action can be brought unless one month's written notice has been given, while Section 272 demands that you must start any action against customs officers within one month of the event.

Marital deceptions

It is possible to insert clauses into private or local bills in the hope that they will be passed into law by Parliament and signed into law without anyone noticing. Back in the days when the position of head of an Oxford college required the holder to be celibate, one college head astonished the fellows by announcing his forthcoming marriage. He pointed to a clause he had had slipped into the local Canal Act, which gave his nuptials legal sanction.

Back in the days when it was only possible to get a divorce by Act of Parliament, an unhappily married town clerk inserted in Clause 64 of a local Waterworks Bill, in between some impenetrable jargon about stopcocks and filter beds, the innocent phrase 'and the Town Clerk's marriage is hereby dissolved'. As no one was still awake by the time they read that far down the Bill, it was enacted. The town clerk was duly divorced; however, when he died and a new town clerk took over, the question arose whether the clause applied only to the previous town clerk or whether any succeeding town clerk was also freed from his marriage vows.

Dead but not buried

When pronouncing a death sentence, it is necessary for the judge to instruct what should happen to the body afterwards. It became standard in the nineteenth century, until the death penalty was abolished in 1965, for the convict's body to be buried within the precincts of the gaol, but in 1840, in a case in Ireland, the judge omitted to mention this. A day or two later, he corrected his error in open court, but not in front of the two men he had condemned. Six out of the ten judges who heard the appeal agreed that the omission rendered the sentence illegal and the two men were pardoned and freed.

All the law entrails

In 1694, a gentleman named Walcott was executed as a traitor. In addition to being hung, drawn and quartered, he received an attainder, which meant that all his property – both real, such as land, and personal – was forfeit to the Crown, and his blood was said to be corrupt, which meant that no title could be passed on to his heirs.

His son sought to have this overturned on the grounds that, when the sentence of hanging, drawing and quartering was passed, the judge omitted to add that the prisoner's entrails would be burned in front of his face. The Crown argued that the hanging, drawing and quartering were the substantive part of the judgement, while the burning of the entrails was only added *in terrorem* – to frighten. In any case, it was 'inconsistent in nature for man to be living after his entrails were taken out of his body'. Nevertheless the King's Bench found in the son's favour.

The King's Bench also said that 'judges are like the officers of the Mint, who must not vary from the standard, either in weight or fineness'. The Crown's contention that sentence could not be carried out – as the condemned man would be dead when his entrails were removed – was dismissed as it was to 'arraign the wisdom and knowledge of all the judges and King's Counsel in all reigns' and the son's counsel pointed to the case of Colonel Harrison, one of Charles I's regicides, who 'was cut down alive, and after his entrails were taken out of his body rose up, and had strength enough left to strike the executioner'.

The case eventually went all the way to the House of Lords, who upheld the decision of the King's Bench – by varying the words, the sentence was illegal. This was little consolation for Walcott Snr. Whether his entrails were in fact burned in front of his face and whether he survived that much of the ordeal is not recorded, but the attainder was lifted and the son's blood uncorrupted, allowing him to inherit.

Getting the charge right

The wording of an indictment has to be precise. In 1823, Thomas Halloway appeared at Hereford Assizes, charged with stealing a brass furnace. In fact, he had stolen the furnace in the neighbouring county of Radnor, broken it up and carried the pieces of brass to Hereford. It was therefore judged that 'though a prisoner may be indicted for a larceny in any county into which he takes stolen property, the present indictment must fail, as he never had the "brass furnace" in Herefordshire … he merely had there pieces of brass'.

Halloway was then indicted for stealing 'two turkeys', but again he got off. Although the evidence showed that he had taken two turkeys from a larder, the judge ruled that the 'two turkeys' in the indictment meant live turkeys. If it had meant dead turkeys, it should have said so.

In a similar case, a man was indicted for stealing 'a pair of stockings', but was acquitted when it was shown that he had taken two odd ones. Another man was acquitted for stealing a duck – when the bird turned out to be a drake.

In 1853, a man was charged with a misdemeanour because he 'did expose … the body and person' on an omnibus. The judge, Mr Justice Maul, questioned this.

'What do you mean in law by exposing his person?' he asked. 'The indictment should have been for exposing his private parts.'

However, the Chief Justice Lord Campbell ruled that, in the Old Bailey at least, the 'person' meant the 'private parts'. Indeed, in the Vagrancy Act of 1824, Parliament had imposed specific penalties against any man 'exposing his person'.

Witnessing wills

The Statute of Frauds of 1677 and the Wills Act of 1837 require that a will be signed, or attested, by the witnesses 'in the presence of' the testator. There have frequently been arguments over what 'in the presence of' means. In 1781, a will was held to be true, even though, as it was a hot day, the testatrix would not come into the lawyer's office to attest the will, preferring to sit in the cool of her carriage outside – it was decided that she could see through the window what was going on. But in a case in 1849, the testator man was in the room when the witnesses signed, but the will was found to be invalid because he had a stiff neck and could not turn his head far enough to actually see the signing.

Signed by hand

By tradition a deed concludes with the words 'signed …' or 'witnessed by my hand'. But this may not be good enough in law. In 1652, a man cut off a dead man's hand, put a pen in it and signed a deed. He then replaced the pen with a seal. Indeed, the court report records that the accused 'signed, sealed and delivered the deed with the dead man's hand, and swore that he saw the deed delivered'. He was fined £100 and made to stand in the pillory for two hours with a notice on his head describing his offence.

CHAPTER ELEVEN

Laughable Libels

VEN THOSE UNCONCERNED with the law are well advised to choose their words carefully for England is famed worldwide for its strict laws on libel and slander. In 1959, Liberace famously won £8,000 libel damages from the *Daily Mirror* after the newspaper implied that he was gay. But there are even more surprising judgements from earlier times.

Curbing the tongue

Under Norman law, a slanderer not only had to pay damages but was also sentenced to stand in the market place of the nearest town, hold his nose between two fingers and declare himself to be a liar. Earlier, in the ninth century, Alfred the Great ordered the tongues of persistent slanderers to be cut out.

A pox on all of you

During the Tudor and Stuart eras, there was a spate of actions for slander, so judges bent over backwards to dismiss cases in an effort to discourage litigation. In 1607 Sir Thomas Holt sued a man named Astgrigg, claiming that he had accused him of being a murderer. The man had said that Holt had 'struck his cook on the head with a cleaver, and cleaved his head: the one part lay on the one shoulder and the other part on the other'. The court decided that this did not constitute an accusation of murder as 'not withstanding such wounding, the party may still be living'.

In 1599, a gentleman named Rutlech said of the future James I: 'Hang him, he is full of pox. I marvel that you will eat or drink with him, I will prove that he is full of the pox.' Again the suit failed. The judge said that the 'pox' in this case did not necessarily mean the 'French pox' – that is, syphilis. It could have meant small pox or cow pox – poxes that implied no stain on a man's moral character. Consequently, the word 'pox' must be taken *in mitiori senu* – in the milder sense.

Similarly, in 1618, a lady named Calford sued a person named Knight for saying: 'Thou art Mutcomb's hackney; thou art a thieving whore, and a pocky whore, and I will prove thee a pocky whore.'

The court ruled that neither the words 'hackney' – a horse that is hired out and, by analogy, a prostitute – nor 'thieving' were actionable as they 'are not any accusation of a felony, for she may be thievish in that which is not a felony'. Again, 'pocky' was not taken necessarily to mean the French pox.

It seems you can call a justice of the peace just about anything you like – a fool, a blockhead, a coxcomb, a bufflehead, an ass – and even, as in one case in 1708, say that he 'knows no more than a slickhill'. Such things may be a 'breach of good behaviour' and you could be bound over to good behaviour, it was decided, but it was not an indictable offence as 'a man cannot help his want of ability, as he may his want of honesty'.

You may call a man a cuckold, but not a wittol – which means a man who is aware or complaisant about the infidelity of his wife – a contented cuckold.

In 1705, it was decided that it was OK to call someone a 'brandy-nosed whore, who stinks of brandy' even though he 'did rather charge the defendant with intemperance and incontinency'.

Gender bending

In 1777, there was a celebrated case over the sex of the Chevalier D'Eon. A man named Da Costa, who bet that the chevalier was in fact a woman, sued the other party to the wager, Jones, for the £300 that had been staked against his 75 guineas – and won the case in court. Side bets worth £75,000 were settled by the verdict. The following year, there was a retrial in front of the same judge, Chief Justice Lord Mansfield, who this time disallowed the action on the grounds of indecency, arguing that you could parade all the indecent evidence you liked on the public stage of a courtroom to prove a criminal case one way or the other, but you could not invade someone's privacy to that extent simply to decide a bet. As it was, the jury in the first trial were wrong – although the chevalier left England in a huff and went to live in Paris in women's clothing, a post-mortem examination in 1810 showed that D'Eon was, anatomically, all man.

Saddled with sin

In 1934, the *News Chronicle* – a popular newspaper of the time – published an article provocatively entitled 'Unchaperoned holidays', which explained how young women of the day had more of a chance to get to know young men if they went off on cycling holidays together.

'In the olden days, a girl's opportunity of meeting men depended largely on how often her mother could entertain,' the article said. 'It was not considered proper for a girl to become acquainted with men outside the house. All that is changed.' Now men and women could spend time alone with each other 'discussing frankly with him many subjects that would have made her parents blush'.

The paper had nothing to illustrate the piece, so they took a picture of two young women on bicycles taken four years previously and substituted a man for one of them. Unfortunately the young lady left in the picture had since married and her husband sued on the grounds that the picture implied that:

Mrs Honeysett had recently been on an unchaperoned holiday with a young man to whom she was not married; that she was a woman of loose morals and low character; that she had committed adultery and was not a fit or proper person to be received in any decent society; and that the male plaintiff [her husband] was unable to exercise any control over his wife, that he was a complacent husband who deserved no respect or sympathy, and one who, through weakness, failed to uphold the dignity of married life.

He was awarded £100 damages.

Smelly feet

In 1937, a policeman sued when an advertisement showed him wiping his brow over the words: 'Phew, I'm going to get my feet into a Jeyes' fluid footbath.' He claimed that this implied he had such 'slovenly and unclean habits' that he needed something especially powerful to 'deodorise or disinfect his feet'.

Under cross-examination he agreed that, after a hard day pounding the beat, a policemen's feet would benefit from a footbath – but 'because they ached, not because they were smelly'. He also utterly refuted the idea that his reputation would be enhanced if he washed his feet in scented bath salts. He was awarded £100 damages.

CHAPTER TWELVE

Parliamentary Peculiarities

 AWS EMANATE FROM Parliament, but the Palace of Westminster itself and its proceedings are bound around by some very strange laws indeed.

Armour

MPs are forbidden to wear armour in Parliament by a law that was passed in 1313 and was designed to stop them coming armed or escorted by armed men, so that debates could be carried out peaceably. And it is still in force today.

No dying

Although it is not technically against the law, no one is allowed to die in Parliament. If anyone has the misfortune to collapse with a fatal heart attack there, the body is removed before the death certificate is issued. This is because the Palace of Westminster is a royal palace and anyone dying in a royal palace is eligible for a state funeral. It is Parliament's status as a royal

palace that allows the bars there to stay open after hours and permits MPs, if they choose, to play roulette in the lobbies.

Duke breaks the law

The House of Lords Precedence Act of 1539 states:

> No person or persons of what estate degree or condition whatsoever he may be of, except only the King's children, shall at any time hereafter attempt to presume to sit or have place at any side of the cloth of estate in the parliament chamber, neither of the one hand of the King's Highness nor of the other, whether the King's Majesty be there personally present or absent.

Clearly this law has been broken on numerous occasions by Prince Philip, the Duke of Edinburgh, who has so far escaped punishment.

It happens each time there is a state opening of Parliament.

In previous reigns, when England had a king instead of a queen, the two thrones under the canopy in the House of Lords at the state opening were occupied by the King and the Prince of Wales or Heiress-Presumptive, while the Queen Consort sat to the left of the King on a chair slightly lower. However, when the present Queen came to the throne, this third chair was removed and Prince Philip sat in the throne formerly occupied by the Prince of Wales. This follows a precedence set by Prince Albert, Queen Victoria's Prince Consort, who was also apparently an habitual offender against Henry VIII's statute.

Dead deputy

During the Second World War an effort was made to amend the Deputy Speaker Act of 1855. Until this Act, the House of Commons could not sit if the Speaker was indisposed. If he died, a new Speaker must be elected and, by custom, taken forcibly to the chair, but if he was unwell or otherwise unable to attend Parliament the sitting was suspended.

Under the Deputy Speaker Act of 1855, though, if the Speaker was not present, for whatever reason, the chairman of the House Ways and Means Committee could sit in his place as Deputy Speaker, with all the procedural powers of the Speaker himself. But wartime brought with it a problem. What would happen if the place where the Speaker was taking shelter was hit by a bomb and it could not be ascertained, possibly for days, whether the Speaker was alive or dead? Could the Deputy Speaker continue in his stead, or would the sitting have to be suspended?

This was a matter of some concern because, during wartime, Acts were being rushed through Parliament and given the Royal Assent within a matter of hours. What would happen if, following an air raid, the Deputy Speaker assumed that the Speaker had survived, a Bill passed both Houses and received the Royal Assent – and then it turned out that the Speaker was dead? The answer was that the Act would be invalid.

As the war was being fought against tyranny on behalf of democracy and the rule of law, this was of some importance. An amendment was drafted in 1941, but no parliamentary time could be found to lay it before the House. Then, early in 1943, the Speaker fell ill and the urgent need to pass the Bill became all to clear. It was scheduled for 3 March 1943, along with a debate on the Navy Estimates, but that very day the Speaker died and the Deputy Speaker was forced to suspend the sitting. In fact, the House was adjourned until the following Tuesday and was out of action for five whole days during wartime.

Strict timekeeping

It was only in 1993 that the Attendance in Parliament Act of 1514 was repealed. This required that no one 'elected to come or be in parliament … depart from the said parliament, nor absent himself from the same, till parliament be fully ended or prorogued … upon pain of … losing all those sums of money which he or they should or ought to have had for his or their wages'.

An even older law, of 1382, which amazingly is still in force, demands that members of both the House of Lords and House of Commons must come when called. Anyone absent without a reasonable or honest excuse 'shall be amerced [fined] or otherwise punished, according as of old times hath been used to be done within the said realm in the said case'.

Law Lords

In the UK, the final arbiter of the law are the Law Lords – a panel of senior judges sitting in the House of Lords. Since the Act of Union in 1801, there have a number of occasions when English law has been determined by a majority of Scottish Law Lords voting down their English counterparts. However, it is more often the case that English Law Lords have determined Scottish law. Until 1921, Irish Law Lords had their say too, and these days South African and Canadian Law Lords sit. The Law Lords are supposed to have a quorum of three, though just two have sat in some cases because there is no one to tell them not to. The Law Lords cannot reverse their own decisions – they have set a precedent and must abide by it. In fact, no court in England can reverse its own decisions – only a higher court can do that.

CHAPTER THIRTEEN

Peculiar Punishments

S PART OF THE BILL OF RIGHTS, the Eighth Amendment to the American Constitution – banning the use of cruel and unusual punishments – was passed into law in 1791. This had become necessary because the English law that the fledgling United States had inherited included some very unpleasant practices.

Mutilation

Before prisons were built in the twelfth century, criminals were mutilated so that they could easily be identified by innocent folk. Anyone who fought with weapons in a church, for example, had an ear cut off, or if he had already lost both his ears was branded on the cheek with a letter 'F'. But help was at hand for those who had been mutilated in this manner. According to Foxe's *Book of Martyrs*, a Befordshire man who had been convicted of theft, having had his eyes pulled out and after suffering terrible mutilation, made his way to the shrine of St Thomas at Canterbury. There, after devout and steadfast prayer, the parts he had lost, we are told, were miraculously restored.

Theft

Chartered boroughs had their own courts and system of punishments. One borough ordinance of 1295 prescribed flogging for the theft of a halfpenny. For stealing between fourpence – 2p – and eightpence-farthing – 4p – the culprit 'shall be set on the pillory and then led to the end of the town and have his ear cut off by the man who caught him'. For thefts of larger amounts, the villain was to be hanged by the man who caught him.

Losing a hand

The practice of mutilation continued into Tudor times. In 1543, Henry VIII passed a law saying that anyone who struck a blow that drew blood within the precincts of the King's palace would have his right hand cut off by members of the royal household. The Serjeant of the Royal Woodyard provided the chopping block, the Master Cook the knife and the Serjeant of the Larder actually cut off the hand; the Serjeant Farrier provided irons to cauterise the stump and afterwards the Serjeant of the Pantry and the Serjeant of the Cellar were on hand with bread and wine – provided the offender could eat and drink left-handed. Chapter 12 of the Act spells out in gruesome detail how the punishment should be carried out:

viii. And for the further declaration of the solemn and due circumstance of the execution appertaining and of long time used and accustomed, to and for such malicious strikings, by reason whereof blood is, hath been, or hereafter shall be shed against the King's peace. It is therefore enacted by the authority aforesaid, that the Sergeant or Chief Surgeon for the time being, or his deputy of the King's household, his heirs and successors, shall be ready at the time and place of execution, as shall be appointed as is aforesaid, to sear the stump when the hand is stricken off.

ix. And the Sergeant of the Pantry shall be also then and there ready to give bread to the party that shall have his hand so stricken off.

x. And the Sergeant of the Cellar shall also be then and there ready with a pot of red wine to give the same party drink after his hand is so stricken off and the stump seared.

xi. And the Sergeant of the Ewry shall also be then and there ready with cloths sufficient for the Surgeon to occupy about the same execution.

xii. And the Yeoman of the Chandry shall also be then and there, and have in readiness cloths sufficient for the Surgeon to occupy about the same execution.

xiii. And the Master Cook shall be also then and there ready, and shall bring with him a dressing-knife, and shall deliver the same knife at the place of execution to the Sergeant of the Larder, who shall be also then and there ready, and hold upright the dressing-knife till the execution be done.

xiv. And the Sergeant of the Poultry shall be also then and there ready with a cock in his hand, ready for the Surgeon to wrap about the same stump, when the hand shall be so stricken off.

xv. And the Yeoman of the Scullery to be also then and there ready, and prepare and make at the place of execution a fire of coals, and there to make ready searing-irons against the said Surgeon or his deputy shall occupy the same.

xvi. And the Sergeant or Chief Farrier shall be also then and there ready, and bring with him the searing-irons, and deliver the same to the same Sergeant or Chief Surgeon or to his deputy when they be hot.

xvii. And the Groom of the Salcery shall be also then and there ready with vinegar and cold water, and give attendance upon the said Surgeon or his deputy until the same execution be done.

xviii. And the Sergeant of the Woodyard shall bring to the said place of execution a block, with a betil, a staple, and cords to bind the said hand upon the block while the execution is in doing.

After all that the one-handed offender was imprisoned for life. This law stayed on the statute books until 1829.

Stocks

Stocks were used in medieval times, the first mention of them in statute being in 1227. Later there were the Stocks Acts of 1350 and 1376, while an Act of 1405 instructed every parish that ran its own affairs to have a set of stocks; a village was downgraded to a mere hamlet if it did not have any stocks. This is another Act that has never been repealed.

Following the Black Death in England in 1349, the Statute of Labourers of 1351 threatened those who refused to work with stocks and branding. And in 1496 Henry VII passed an Act that stated: 'It is enacted that vagabonds, idle and suspected persons, shall be set in the stocks three days and three nights, and have none other sustenance than bread and water, and then shall be put out of the town.'

Second offenders were given six days and six nights, although Henry VIII reduced this in 1504 to one day and one night, while an Act of 1624 offered a financial alternative: pay a fine of one shilling – 5p – or spend three hours in the stocks.

Whipping

English law has always been tough on the poor. An Act of 1530 complained that 'vagabonds and beggars have a long time increased and daily do increase in great and excessive numbers by the occasion of idleness, mother and root of all vices, whereby had upsurged and sprung up ... continual thefts and murders, and other heinous offences and great enormities'. Vagrants were stripped and flogged through the streets at the back of a cart. However, as the numbers were swelled with wounded soldiers and sailors, cripples who could not earn a productive living were allowed to apply to the local justices for a licence to beg.

But it was not just the poor who suffered, for corporal punishment was even introduced to the universities. In 1583, a loud-mouthed apprentice, convicted for chatting 'undutifully' about the conduit in Fleet Street, was 'stripped naked from hys gyrdle upward' and given 'twelve strypes with a rodd at the poste of reformacon' next to the conduit. These 'postes of reformacion', or whipping posts, began to appear all over London. Women too were stripped to the waist for whipping and the order often specified that the whipping continued 'till her body be bloody'.

In 1596 an Act of Parliament officially authorised whipping posts, and 'incorrigible rogues' were sent to Houses of Correction, where they were chained and whipped. But this failed to stop the increasing tide of: 'Abraham men' who pretended to be mad having just been released from Bedlam; 'counterfeit cranks' who feigned epilepsy, using a piece of soap to make themselves foam at the mouth; 'dommerars' who pretended to be dumb; 'upright men' who got a job to steal from their employers; 'freshwater mariners' who pretended to be the survivors of sunken ships; 'glimmers' who carried fake testimonials saying their houses had been burned down; 'bawdy baskets' who stole linen that was hung out to dry; and the original 'hookers' who used long poles with hooks on to steal things through open windows.

Gradually public sentiment turned against public flogging but it was not until 1780 that public whipping was confined to the streets outside the Old Bailey and the Middlesex session house. A poem of the time told that 'West End dandies paid a visit daily, To see the strumpets whipped at the Old Bailey'. Public flogging for women was finally abolished in 1817 and for men a decade later.

Branding

While branding was common in continental Europe, in England it was usually only the hand that was burned. When a felon escaped the gallows by successfully pleading 'by benefit of clergy', their thumbs were branded, so that they could not make the same plea twice, although sometimes the face was disfigured. In the fifteenth century, anyone found with goods stolen from a church in Dover would be branded on the forehead with the church key.

In November 1556, the chronicler John Stow recorded that 'a man was brought from Westminster Hall riding with his face to the horse tail, and a paper on his head, to the Standard in Cheape, & there set on the pillorie, and then burned with an hote yron on both his cheekes, with two letters "F" and "A" for False Accusing one of the court of Comon place [Common Pleas] in Westminster of treason'.

Such events were rare, though the law made provision for the widespread use of branding. An Act of 1547 said that sturdy beggars should be enslaved and 'marked with a whott iron in the brest with the marke of V'. This was so rarely enforced that another Act was passed in 1572, under which vagrants were to be 'burnte through the gristle of the right eare with a hot yron of the compasse of an ynch about'. Gangs of vagrants were branded this way, but in 1581 the Act aroused opposition when an East Tilbury husbandman protested that 'ther is no christian prince that hathe suche crewell laws as to burne men throwe their eares which are nowe used in this Realme'. This Act was finally repealed in 1593.

Branding itself was abolished in 1822, though it had not been used since 1706.

Cheating tradesmen

Dishonest tradesmen were paraded through the streets with a symbol of their offence. In 1517, a butcher was ordered to ride through the City of London with two sides of bacon tied to him, two flitches carried before him, a paper attached to his head and basins being banged to attract attention 'ffor puttyng to sale of mesell [measle or diseased] and stynkyng bacon'.

For repeated convictions the offender was also sentenced to the pillory. In 1560 a crooked butcher from Theydon in Essex was 'sett in the pyllory in Cheapesyde ... with the sayd bacon hanginge about him and over his hedde uppon the saide pyllorrye, and a paper affyxed to the seyd pyllorie declarynge not only this his sayd offence, but also the like offence by him here comytted in the tyme of the mayraltye of Sir Thomas Leigh'.

Overcharging was considered an even graver offence, especially if the perpetrator had the temerity to overcharge the royal household. Soon after Elizabeth I came to the throne,

one of the takers of freshe fishe for the provision of the Queenes house was set on the Pillorie in Cheape side in the fishe market over agaynst the kings head, having a bauldrike [necklace] of smeltes hanging about his necke with a paper on his foreheade, written 'for buying smelts for .xij. pens a hundred, and solde them againe for ten pens a quarter'.

He was to stand in the pillory for three hours on three days, then 'on the last day he should have had one of his eares slitte, if by great suyte made to the Counsayle by the Lorde Mayor of London, he hadde not beene pardoned'.

Magistrates were quite imaginative in making the punishment fit the crime. In 1478, a man convicted of illegally tapping a conduit to fill his own well was ordered to be paraded on horseback 'with a vessell like unto a conduyt full of water uppon his hede, the same water running by smale pipes oute of the same vessell and that when the water is wasted newe water to be put in the said vessell ageyn'.

In 1535 a gongfarmer – a lavatory cleaner – was ordered to

stand 'yn one of hys owne pypes [barrels]... yn fylthe with a paper upon hys hed for castying of ordure yn the open stretes'.

Backwards riding

Cheating wood-sellers were ridden around with billets of wood slung around their necks, and in 1553 a pair of coal merchants from Edgware and Croydon were ridden around sitting back to front on horseback with 'a sak of their coles hagynge aboute their neck, the one ende of the same sakkes with the one half of the coll hangynge at their bakk & thother ende with thother half of the coll hangyne on their brest'.

Back-to-front riding was a popular punishment at that time. In 1537, a minstrel was punished for keeping a woman disguised in 'mannes rayment', and was ordered to ride through the city 'on horsebakke with his fact to the horse tayll with a paper on hys hedde & to play up hys owne instrument afore her'.

For slandering James I's daughter and her husband, the Elector Palatine and the deposed King of Bohemia, along with various other dignitaries, Edward Floyd was sentenced in 1621 to ride 'from Westminster then to the Fleete with his face to the horse tayle and the tayle in his hand, with a paper on his forehead'.

The pillory

The pillory was introduced in Anglo-Saxon times to punish slander, using loaded dice or begging with someone else's child. Under the Normans it came to be the traditional punishment for tradesmen who had cheated their customers – particularly a butcher who sold bad meat or a greengrocer who gave short weight. It was similar to the stocks, but instead of restraining the victim's ankles, a hinged wooden frame held him by the neck and wrists; spectators were then allowed to pelt the victim with anything that came to hand. Villains feared it more than any fine, imprisonment and even the lash. Titus Oates, the instigator of the Popish Plot of 1678, almost died from the brickbats thrown at him in the pillory.

Ears were in constant danger in the pillory. In London in 1502 a notorious pickpocket had his right ear lopped off while he was in the pillory. That same day, the writer and publisher of seditious tales against the King and nobles was to have both his ears cut off.

Culprits' ears were often nailed to the pillory, with the nails being pulled out with pincers at the end of the punishment, though in one case in London in 1552 it was ordered that the culprit 'shall pluck it [the ear] from the pyllorie hym selfe att his goinge downe withoute the helpe of eny other or els remayne there styll'.

That same year a 'gentleman' who had had his ear nailed to the pillory in Cheapside for obtaining goods by deceit stayed in the pillory until after midnight rather than pull himself free at the risk of losing it. It did him no good as a helpful beadle 'slitted yt upwards with a penknife' while freeing him.

But the threat of ear damage was usually enough. Again in 1552, a wax chandler was sentenced to spend three market days in the pillory 'for slanderous rayllyng upon my lord the mayer & his brethren th'aldermen'. But even on the pillory he protested his innocence, so he was ordered to admit his guilt publicly or suffer 'hys eares upon the rest of th'execucion of hys seid judgement to be cutt of openly upon the pyllore'. He promptly recanted and was discharged.

Under the Forgery Act of 1562 the punishment became more brutal. A convicted forger had to repay the aggrieved party double their costs and damages, 'and shall also be set upon a pillory in some open market town, or other open place, and there to have both his ears cut off, and also his nostrils to be slit and cut, and seared with irons, so as they may remain for a perpetual note or mark of his falsehood'. And then they had to forfeit all their land and go to prison for life.

Under a statute of James 1 in 1623, anyone unfortunate enough to go bankrupt was nailed by one ear to the pillory for two hours, and then had the ear cut off. In 1731, 70-year-old forger Joseph Cook underwent the full terrible punishment while he stood in the pillory at Charing Cross.

'Not fit to be looked upon'

The pillory was dangerous enough without added mutilations. In 1732, Mrs Beare was sent to the pillory in Derby for inciting another woman to poison her husband and murder her child. The officers found she had a large pewter plate under her headdress – when it was removed she was pelted with such a shower of eggs, turnips, potatoes and the like that she was not expected to live. She lost a great deal of blood and those who saw her afterwards in gaol said that she was 'such an object as was not fit to be looked upon'.

In 1751, four men were found guilty of falsely accusing innocent people of theft for reward money and were so badly treated in the pillory 'that Egan was struck dead in less than half-an-hour, and Salmon was so dangerously wounded that it was through impossible for him to recover'. And in 1777, Ann Morrow, who dressed up as a man and married three different women, was 'pelted ... to such a degree, that she lost the sight of both eyes'.

The pillory was abolished as a punishment for most crimes in 1817, although it remained the punishment for riot and perjury until 1837.

Daniel Defoe

Early in his career, the author of *Robinson Crusoe*, Daniel Defoe, was sentenced to the pillory. At the end of the seventeenth century, Nonconformists were being driven from public life and Defoe, a dissenter, struck back with a satirical pamphlet entitled *The Shortest Way with the Dissenters* – meaning to kill them all – which he published anonymously. It sold well, but no one saw the joke. Both dissenters and high churchmen took it seriously and were outraged when the hoax was exposed.

All too aware of the consequences, Defoe went into hiding. After weeks on the run, Defoe was finally arrested, charged with seditious libel and sent to Newgate, the most dreaded of London's 27 gaols. His trial at the Old Bailey attracted a huge crowd who paid a shilling a head to see Defoe in the dock.

The outcome of the trial was a forgone conclusion. The judges on the bench were men who Defoe had lampooned in earlier pamphlets, saying that they took bribes, always favoured the rich over the poor, and at least two of them enjoyed seeing prostitutes they themselves had used being stripped and whipped in Bridewell jail.

Found guilty, Defoe was sentenced to three days in the pillory. He could have mitigated his sentence by naming his accomplices, but instead he wrote *Hymn to the Pillory*, another satire defaming his enemies, including the very judges who had sentenced him. It was on sale as he stood in the pillory outside the Royal Exchange on 29 July 1703 and continued to do brisk business when he stood in the pillory at Cheapside the following day and at Temple Bar on the last day of the month. His defiance was rewarded – people liked his pamphlet so much that, on all three days, he was surrounded by cheering crowds and the only thing he was pelted with were flowers.

Although Defoe made money from the sale of his *Hymn to the Pillory*, his judges took their revenge by detaining him in gaol until the brickworks he owned in Tilbury went bankrupt. After that, he was forced to concentrate all his energies on his literary career.

The cucking stool

Women were rarely sentenced to the pillory, though in late medieval London there was a version of the pillory called the 'thew', specifically for women. By 1500, this seems to have been replaced by the cucking stool, which was designed to expose female offenders to public shame rather than immersion. Later the cucking stool became the ducking stool.

In 1529 seven 'common women', probably prostitutes, were sentenced 'to be had to the cukkyng stole', though it is not clear if they were ducked. However, in 1535 a group of 'myghty vagabond and wys-women of theyre bodyes' were taken to Smithfield and 'sett upon the cukkying stooe & ... wasshed over the eares'. By 1577, William Harrison noted in his *Description of England* that 'harlots and their mates, by carting, ducking, and dooing of open penance ... are often put to rebuke'. Harrison also mentioned that 'scolds', or quarrelsome women, were 'ducked upon cucking stooles in the water'.

Harsher penalties still were inflicted for sexual offences. As in the Isle of Man, there was 'the dragging of some of them over the Thames between Lambeth and Westminster at the taile of a boat ... this was inflicted upon them by none other than the knight marshal, and that within the compasse of his jurisdiction & limits onelie' – that is, within the royal court and its environs. This was because the cucking stool itself, in some cases, did not prove much of a deterrent.

Baptism or murder?

Men sometimes got a soaking too. In 1646, Samuel Oates was travelling through Essex, preaching and baptising the multitudes. One of his new-found flock, a woman named Ann, died a few weeks later, the cause of death, it was thought, being dipped in cold water.

Oates was arrested, put in fetters and thrown into gaol. When he came to trial the prosecution maintained that he had held the woman 'so long in the water that she fell presently sick, became swelled and died in a fortnight; and on her deathbed blamed the dipping'. However, a defence witness said that Ann was in better health after the baptism than before and a verdict of not guilty was returned.

But the mob were not satisfied, dragged Oates to a nearby pump and drenched him. Then they threw him in the river.

Scolds

Scolding was outlawed by statute in 1585. This was an offence that applied primarily, but not exclusively, to women, particularly troublesome women who caused a nuisance by using ribald or abusive language. They would be 'exposed' on the scold's cart which trundled around town to shame them. A persistent scold could be silenced with a scold's bit, which fitted in the mouth, but the most barbaric punishment was the scold's bridle, a metal cage that completely enclosed the head. It originated in Scotland and, although its use was widespread, it was never sanctioned by statute.

Usually the punishment was less harsh. In fourteenth-century London, scolds or brawlers had to carry a 'dystaff with towen' – flax. A distaff was a rod for holding flax, tow or wool while spinning and the punishment was to remind them to be more womanly in their ways.

It seems that Ann Walker got off particularly lightly when she came up before the judge at Wakefield Quarter Sessions on 4 October 1614 for calling Andrew Shaw a 'cuckoo'. She was found guilty and the sentence handed down was that 'the Constable of Wakefield shall cause the said Ann Walker, for her impudent and bold behaviour, to be runge through the town with basins before her, as is accustomed for common scoldes.' This meant she was paraded through town behind people bashing metal basins together like cymbals to draw attention to her.

But more commonly the punishment was the ducking stool. Most village ponds once boasted one and women found guilty of scolding were sentenced to be dunked in the pond, a practice that continued into the nineteenth century. A magistrate in Leominster sentenced a woman to be ducked in 1817, but the water in the pond was too low and she was wheeled around town in the ducking chair instead.

Scolding continued to be a crime until 1967, when the Criminal Law Act abolished 'any distinct offence under common law in England and Wales of maintenance (including champerty, but not embracery), challenging to fight, eavesdropping or being a common barrator, a common scold or a common night walker'.

Prostitutes

London ordinances of the fourteenth century say that 'common women', or prostitutes, should be paraded wearing hoods made of ray – striped material – with a white wand in their hands. The parade was led through the city by minstrels, playing raucous tunes on musical instruments, and sometimes metal basins were beaten or other 'vile minstrelsy' was employed.

In 1519 three common strumpets were convicted for the 'abhomynacion' of cutting their hair short like men, so that they could wear men's clothing, presumably to drum up the transvestite trade. They were ordered to be paraded through the streets with white wands in their hands, ray hoods about their shoulders and wearing 'mennes bonett on their hed, without eny kercher [kerchief or scarf], their hed kemte [kempt or combed]'.

Bad hair day

A fourteenth-century ordinance of the City of London read: 'If any woman shall be found to be a common receiver of courtesans or bawd ... let her be openly bought, with minstrels, from prison to the thew, and set thereon for a certain time ... and there let her hair be cut round about her head.' Prostitutes suffered the same penalties for a third offence. In 1559, two 'auncyent and commen harlottes of their bodies' were to be carted through the streets with ray hoods, white wands, basins banging and the rest of it, to the pillory and 'their here to be cutt & shavyn above their eares'.

Male sexual misconduct was similarly punished: 'If any

man shall be found to be a common whoremonger or bawd … let all the head and beard be shaved except a fringe on the head, two inches in breadth; and let him be taken unto the pillory, with minstrels, and set there for a certain time'.

In 1510, the London Court of Aldermen ordered two pimps to have 'their head to be polled [sheared or shaved] above the eyes and the same day in markett season to be ledde from thens to the pillorie in Cornhull thervppon to stande by the space of an houre', while in 1561 a man and his half-sister convicted of incest were ridden around the city for three market days, 'havying their heare shorne above their eares … for a deformitie'.

Transportation

Transportation to the plantations in the West Indies or North America was practised on an ad hoc basis throughout the seventeenth century, particularly after the Restoration in 1660, although it fell out of use in the 1670s as planters only wanted strong and fit young men. After the Civil War, England was underpopulated and could scarcely afford to lose the most able-bodied.

In 1717, George I included a clause in the Piracy Act allowing the transportation of various thieves and unlawful exporters of wool. The following year the punishment was extended to those killing deer. The period of exile was usually seven or 14 years, with anyone returning before that time being executed.

Other offences were added. In 1751, the punishment for stealing the bodies of the executed was seven years in the Americas. Two years later those marrying unlawfully in places other than churches or chapels, or without a licence or reading the banns, got 14 years on the plantations. Later still, perjury, obtaining money by false pretences and stealing from black-lead mines and bleaching grounds were added. Convicts were sold to shipowners for £3, and later £5, who sold them on to plantation owners for £10, though women only fetched £8.

The trade was hampered by the Seven Years' War between 1756 and 1763. Then, as the slave trade flourished, plantation owners preferred to buy Africans who were usually stronger, were better suited to the climate and were theirs for life. This left England's gaols overcrowded, so in 1768 George III tried to revive the arrangement with a new Transportation Act, which the British saw as an enlightened peace of legislation as it included a pardon, provided the person transported did not return to Britain within their period of transportation.

The 1768 Act was well timed – seven years later the American War of Independence broke out and George III lost his plantations there, but in 1770, Captain Cook landed in Australia and in 1786 the British government began building a penal colony at Botany Bay.

There were numerous candidates for transportation. At that time capital offences in Great Britain included: arson, beast-stealing, burglary, coining, forgery, highway robbery, horse- and sheep-stealing, house-breaking, manslaughter, murder, privately stealing, rape, rioting, robbery in a dwelling house, robbing the mails, robbing the post office, shoplifting, stealing in a dwelling house, stealing on board a ship or barge, treason and unlawful shooting. Stealing anything in any circumstances worth more than £1 19s 0p – £1.90 – was a capital offence. But stealing something below the same limit could also be a capital offence if there were any aggravating circumstances. House-breaking – that is, breaking and entering – counted as a double felony no matter how little was taken and was, consequently, a capital offence. And if a prostitute took a shilling from her client's pocket during the performance of her trade, this again was a double felony.

However, judges and juries were no longer willing to send criminals to the gallows for trivial offences and were particular unwilling to convict women. So with the connivance of the court double felonies became single felonies, punished merely by transportation, usually for seven years. Even when women were convicted of capital offences, the judge would draw up a petition for pardon and commute the sentence to 'transportation to parts beyond the seas'. It was not uncommon for men and women to be transported for seven years for as little as stealing a loaf of bread.

The first convict ship arrived in Sydney Cove in 1788, carrying 736 prisoners. Although convicts were used as forced labour, often in chain gangs and punished by flogging, the system was criticised in Britain for its leniency as well as its inefficiency. It certainly proved no deterrent as crime continued to soar. After an inquiry by a select committee of the House of Commons in 1837, the British government decided to stop transportation and it was abolished in 1857, although convicts sentenced to penal servitude continued to be sent to Western Australia until 1867. The last convict ship arrived in Fremantle in 1868, carrying 279 prisoners. In all, some 137,000 men and 25,000 women were transported to Australia. By contrast, the French continued to use transportation as a punishment until 1938.

Debtors' prisons

In 1716, there were over 60,000 people in gaol for debt in England and Wales. In most parts of the country there were no separate prisons for debtors, but in London there were three – the Fleet, the Marshalsea and the King's Bench. The Fleet, near Blackfriars, had existed since the twelfth century and had once been a royal prison, housing those who had been convicted by the Star Chamber. It was notorious for its turnkeys who extorted money from the inmates, often making it impossible for them to pay their debts and leave. Famous inmates include founder of the Society of Friends, George Fox, founder of Pennsylvania, William Penn, William Hogarth's father and John Cleland, who wrote *Fanny Hill* in the Fleet where he was incarcerated for debt between 1748 and 1752. John Donne spent time there in 1602 when, at the age of 29, he contracted a secret marriage to a minor, 16-year-old Ann More.

Prostitution and drunkenness were rife and there were notorious Fleet marriages, often involving minors, conducted without banns or a licence by penurious priests. The Fleet was also a well-known receiving house for smuggled or stolen goods as the excise men were too afraid of the inmates to search the place.

The Marshalsea, on the south side of the Thames, became home to the public executioner, John Price, who lived above his means and had run up debts of 7s 6d (38p). After three years, he escaped by breaking through the wall, murdered an old woman and was hanged by his successor.

The King's Bench prison was nearby. Goldsmith and Garrick visited Tobias Smollett there in 1759, while the MP John

Wilkes was sentenced to 22 months there and fined £1,000 for obscene and seditious libel. On his way from Westminster Hall to the King's Bench prison on 10 May, a crowd of his supporters gathered, the Riot Act was read and the Third Regiment of Foot Guards opened fire on the mob, killing several people in what became know as the 'St George's Fields Massacre'.

While the poor lived in appalling conditions in the prison, often for a very long time, the rich were able to rent an apartment where they could live with their wives and families. The keeper of the Fleet charged £2 4s 6d for a room on the 'gentleman's side', the official charge being 4d.

Naturally Wilkes lived in style in the King's Bench. Friends and relations brought pork, salmon, game and wine, and paid his fines. He was also visited by his mistress, Mrs Bernard, and enjoyed the favours of other young women. In 1776, some 78 prisoners lived in private houses that were actually outside the prison walls, while 241 lived inside in considerable squalor.

Prison reformer John Howard complained that many debtors made a mockery of the law by living as comfortably in prison as they did at home, with no incentive whatever to pay their debts. By contrast, poorer prisoners were clapped in irons, or thrown into cells with prisoners suffering from smallpox or into dungeons over sewers filled with corpses.

In 1792, a scandal erupted after a woman died in a Devon gaol after 45 years imprisonment for a debt of £19. After that the Thatched House Society set to work ransoming debtors by paying their debts, over the next 20 years freeing 12,590 debtors at an average cost of £2 5s 0d – £2.25 – a head.

Both the Fleet and King's Bench prisons were completely destroyed by the Gordon Riots of 1780, though they were rebuilt. The Marshalsea had been moved a little to the south when Charles Dickens' father was confined there for a debt of £40 in 1824. Debtors' prisons appear in *Pickwick Papers*, *David Copperfield* and *Little Dorrit*.

The Marshalsea and Fleet prisons were closed in 1842 and the King's Bench – by then called the Queen's Bench – became a military prison after imprisonment for civil debt was abolished. It was demolished in 1879.

Newgate

While debtors went to the Fleet, Marshalsea and the King's Bench prisons, and traitors went to the Tower of London, ordinary criminals languished in Newgate, which existed as a prison from the 1100s to 1903, when it was finally demolished. The Old Bailey stands on the site today.

It was a hellhole, with typhus – or gaol fever – killing many before the hangman got around to them. In 1414, 40 prisoners and one gaoler died of gaol fever in a single week. The poor lived in absolute darkness and slept on vermin-ridden straw. They competed with rats for the stale bread thrown to them and lice crunched underfoot as prisoners moved about. The smell was so bad that people walking by in the street would hold nosegays to their faces to avoid the stench.

The better off could comfort themselves with beer and gin, which was sold by the gaolers at exorbitant prices. Pigs, pigeons and other pets could be kept in the cells up to 1792 and, until Victorian times, accommodation was mixed. In those days, trials were swift and execution or transportation occurred soon after, although sometimes there were oversights. In 1689, Major John Bernardi was imprisoned in Newgate, but somehow his case slipped through the net and he was held there for the next 47 years until he died, still awaiting trial. During that time, he and his wife had ten children.

CHAPTER FOURTEEN

Die Laughing

 ITH THE PASSING OF THE Human Rights Act in 1998, the death penalty has now been abolished for all offences under English law. Yet for centuries the judicial system indulged itself in inflicting death in a number of strange and usual ways.

Boiling alive

Henry VIII was a bloodthirsty tyrant. During his 38-year reign he had over 70,000 people executed – an average of over five people a day. But he wanted something particularly gruesome to punish John Roose, who had been convicted of putting poison in a pot of broth intended for the family of the Bishop of Rochester and for the poor of the parish. In 1530 Henry passed a special Act to have Roose boiled alive. In 1542, Margaret Davey suffered the same terrible fate in Smithfield. After a third case, Edward VI passed a law making all wilful poisoning the regular felony of murder, although Henry VIII's original Act still remained on the statute book until 1863.

Murdered child

Punishments north of the border could be just as gruesome. When Margaret Alexander was convicted of murdering her two illegitimate children by Patrick Learmonth, she was forced to dig up the body of her second child from the churchyard, carry it in a public procession around town to the brewhouse where she had given birth, then to the place on the river back where she had originally dug a hole to hide the child's body. After publicly confessing her crimes, she was hanged and her arms were cut off. One was displayed in Haddington and the other at Aberlady, where she had given birth to the first murdered child.

Beheading

Beheading was not practised in England before Norman times – the first man to have his head chopped off was Walthoef, Earl of Northumberland, in 1075. During the reign of Henry IV, it was made illegal for sheriffs to behead someone who had been sentenced to hang.

Men beheading badly

Those condemned to be beheaded in England were advised to tip the axeman generously so that he would sharpen his blade and ensure that the job was done with one blow.

The best executioner was said to have been a man called Derick, who gave his name to the tower of an oil rig or the hoist used on board ship which is shaped like a gallows. The worst is said to have been Richard Jaquet, also known as Jack Ketch, whose sobriquet has been attached to all those who followed his trade.

In 1683, when William Russell was condemned for plotting to kill Charles II, he paid Ketch 20 guineas – £21 – to make a good job of it. But when the first blow of the axe glanced off the side of his neck, Russell said, 'You dog. Did I pay you to treat me so inhumanely?' It took three further blows to sever the head and Ketch was jeered from the scaffold.

Two years later, Ketch was employed to behead the Duke of Monmouth. After four blows, the head was still in place and he had to finish the job with a knife. The following year, Ketch

was sacked and was replaced by a man named Pascha Rose who, after only a few months in the job, was arrested for murder and hanged. Ketch got his old job back.

Hanging, drawing and quartering

The dreaded punishment of hanging, drawing and quartering was only abolished on 4 July 1870, though it had long fallen into disuse. The victim was strung up by the neck and partially hanged, then castrated and disembowelled while still alive; his entrails were burned in front of his face and his body was cut into four. This terrible punishment was inflicted because, in a time when life could be unpleasant, brutish and short, to be despatched swiftly with a blow from an axe was no deterrent.

Originally the body was cut into four quarters so that the pieces could to taken to the four corners of the country to demonstrate the fate of traitors, but eventually the body parts were distributed around Temple Bar, the City Gates and the Tower of London.

On 13 October 1660, Samuel Pepys wrote: 'I went out to Charing Cross to see Major-General Harrison' – one of the regicides – 'hanged, drawn and quartered, which was done there, he was looking as cheerful as any man could do in that condition. He was presently cut down, and his head and heart shown to the people, at which there was great shouts of joy.'

On 20 October, he wrote: 'This afternoon going through London and called at Crowe's, the upholster's in St Bartholomew's, I saw the limbs of some of our new traitors set upon Aldersgate, which was a sad sight to see; and a bloody week this and the last have been, there being ten hanged, drawn and quartered.'

The practice of displaying the severed head on a pike on top of the Tower of London or on London Bridge was ended in the 1700s. The last people to be beheaded were the Cato Street Conspirators who planned to assassinate the Cabinet in 1820. They were 'drawn' too, but not by having their entrails drawn out of them – rather they were drawn to the scaffold on a hurdle.

Burning

Women were not hanged, drawn and quartered, the law recognising that 'the decency due to the sex forbids the exposing and publicly mutilating their bodies'. Instead they would be dragged to the gallows and burned alive. Attorney-General Sir Edward Coke said, 'It is punishment undoubtedly just, for our liege lord the King is lord of every one of our members, and they have severally conspired against him, and should each one suffer.'

Usually burning was reserved for heretics, but women found guilty of murdering their husbands or masters – an offence known as petty treason – were also burned at the stake. In the early days the prisoner would be burned alive while still conscious. By the time of Mary I, the woman would be burned naked, but was permitted to have a bag of gunpowder tied around her neck to hasten death. Later, as an act of mercy, the prisoner was strangled first.

The last burning took place in 1789 and the practice was formally abolished in 1790.

The gibbet

There were gibbets on all the roads into London at Kensington, Knightsbridge, Hampstead, Highgate, Finchley, Wimbledon and Putney, and outside most cities and county towns. Bodies were left there to rot as a warning to others. To slow the process they were covered with tar, although this made it easy for friends and relatives of the culprit to set fire to the corpse. The last corpse to be left hanging from a gibbet in chains was outside Leicester in 1832 and the practice formally abolished in 1834.

Tyburn

The traditional place of execution was at Jack Ketch's Tree at Tyburn, where Marble Arch now stands, though there were also gallows in Soho Square, Bloomsbury Square, Smithfield, St Giles in Holborn, Blackheath, Kennington Common and on City Road in Islington.

The first person to be executed at Tyburn was William 'Longbeard' Fitzobert, in 1196, who led a rebellion against the tax being levied to ransom Richard the Lionheart from Henry VI of Austria. When the rebellion failed, William sought sanctuary in St Mary-le-Bow in the City of London, but the Archbishop of Canterbury, Hubert de Burgh, who was also Justiciary of the Kingdom (prime minister and chief justice rolled into one) ordered his men to set fire to the church to force Longbeard out.

The first permanent gallows built at Tyburn in 1571 were a 'triple tree' – a gallows with three beams, each to accommodate eight people so that the executioner could hang 24 people at a time. During the reign of James I, around 150 people were hanged annually, but by the 1700s this had risen to up to 40 a day, with Tyburn fairs being held every six weeks.

Criminals were bought from Newgate by cart – notorious criminals often dressed up for the occasion as if going to a wedding. Their first stop was the Church of St Sepulchre, where the bell was tolled and they were given a bunch of posies. At the Church of St Giles-in-the-Field they were given a jug of ale and they stopped at every pub on the way, famously at the Bowl Inn in St Giles's and the White Hart on Drury Lane. Each publican gave them a free drink, as the condemned men and women would bring in the crowds – this is the origin of the expression 'one for road'. Victims often joked that they would pay on the way back.

Hampered by huge crowds, the procession along Oxford Road, now Oxford Street, could take hours. Popular prisoners were showered with flowers, while unpopular ones were pelted with rotten vegetables and stones. There would be a carnival atmosphere with the crowds singing and chanting, and street vendors selling gingerbread, gin and oranges.

Around the gallows there were wooden stands, where spectators paid 2s 0d – 10p – for a good view. The largest stand with the best view was Old Mother Proctor's Pews, after Mother Proctor who owned them.

A priest would say a prayer and the condemned were invited to publicly confess their crimes. Some gave long speeches in self-justification; others seized the moment to abuse the authorities, the hangman, the priest or the crowd. Then the noose was put around their necks and the hangman whipped the horses to pull away the cart and leave the condemned dangling. After half an hour, the bodies were cut down.

The hangman was entitled to keep their clothes. In 1447, five men were stripped ready for hanging when their pardons came through. The hangman refused to return their clothes and they had to walk home naked. The bodies also belonged to the hangman. Although he was obliged to sell those of murderers to surgeons for dissection, he sometimes sold them back to their families, if they offered a better price. Sometimes it was difficult to keep the corpse intact as the crowd would try to grab parts as souvenirs. The hangman would also cut up the rope and sell bits of it in the pubs of Fleet Street.

The Anatomy Act

An Act of Parliament of 1540 gave schools of anatomy four corpses of executed prisoners every year on which to practise. However, as the demand for fresh corpses provided a ready market for grave-robbers – known as 'sack-'em-up' men – a new Act in 1752 gave schools of anatomy the bodies of all hanged murderers. This added a further deterrent to the death sentence because people then believed they would not be resurrected into the life hereafter if they had not been buried intact – but it did not stop the trade in corpses. In Edinburgh in 1827 and 1828, William Burke and William Hare were charging over £8 each from Professor Robert Knox for bodies, no questions asked. Then, in 1831, Messrs Bishop, May and Williams murdered an Italian beggar boy in Bethnal Green, London and tried to sell the body to King's College, as a result of which the 1832 Anatomy Act was passed. This allowed any corpse to be legally dissected, provided its owner had not expressly objected while alive – and it put the sack-'em-up men out of business.

The end of public hanging

In the second half of the eighteenth century, the area around Tyburn became a smart residential district and after 1783 executions were restricted to Newgate, where they were still a popular form of entertainment. In 1840 it cost £25 to rent a window with a good view and the keeper of Newgate gaol would entertain distinguished guests with a lavish breakfast of devilled kidneys and brandy on execution days.

One morning in the spring of 1818 the artist George Cruikshank, who illustrated many of the books of Charles Dickens, was strolling in the City when he came across the gallows with corpses still hanging. Two of the bodies belonged to young women who looked barely older than sixteen. When he asked a bystander what the girls had done, he was told that they been hanged for trying to forge a £1 note.

Shocked, Cruikshank drew on a £1 note of his own a row of corpses hanging from a gallows where the head of Queen Victoria should be. When his drawing was published it caused outrage. The Bank of England even had to stop issuing £1 notes for a time and, under public pressure, the Home Secretary Sir Robert Peel was forced to abolish the death penalty for minor crimes in 1832.

Public hangings were ended in 1868, with the last one outside Newgate on 26 May that year. The man hanged was a terrorist called Michael Barratt who had blown up the Clerkenwell House of Detention, killing six people.

Hanging from the yardarm

The last man to be hanged from the yardarm under naval law was Private John Dalinger of the Royal Marines on 13 July 1860. He was serving aboard HMS *Leven* in Talienwan Bay, China and had been convicted of attempting to murder his captain. This was the last time an execution took place on a ship of the Royal Navy.

Odd offences

A comprehensive statute of 1722 made it a capital offence to: hunt and kill deer; destroy the heads of fishponds; steal rabbits from warrens; destroy trees growing in avenues and gardens; set fire to haystacks and houses; shoot at a person, even if the shot missed; extort money; or rescue any person held in custody. Other capital offences included: taking false oaths to receive a seaman's pay; 'being disguised within the Mint'; damaging Westminster and other bridges; making false entries in the marriage register; impersonating out-pensioners of Greenwich Hospital; or being seen in the company of gypsies. By 1800 there were some 200 capital offences on the statute books.

In the 1750s, two-thirds of those convicted in London and Middlesex were actually hanged, but as transportation and being confined to ship hulks were introduced, that number dropped to below one-third.

The age of criminal responsibility was seven and children were routinely executed. In 1814, on one day alone five children aged between eight and 14 were sentenced to death at the Old Bailey. In 1833, a nine-year-old boy was sentenced to death for stealing paint worth tuppence-h'apenny from a shop, while a 12 year old was transported for seven years for stealing two penny rolls, and a 13 year old was transported for life after taking a companion's hat when they were watching a puppet show.

Gradually the use of capital punishment was phased out. In 1864, 1,066 people in England and Wales were sentenced to death, but only 49 were actually executed. By 1863, 29 were sentenced and 22 executed.

The long drop

The old-fashioned method of hanging was the 'short drop' which left the victim to strangle slowly after the cart had moved away and took 30 minutes or more. Friends and relatives would often pull on the victim's feet to hasten the process. The improved 'long drop' method that instantly broke the victim's neck when they fell through a trap door was introduced when public hangings moved to Newgate in 1783, but it did not take over completely.

The famous hangman William Calcraft, who held office from 1829 until 1874, still favoured the short-drop method and would hang onto his victim's legs if he thought their death was coming too slowly. His successor William Marwood reintroduced the long-drop method, and it was turned into a precise science by James Berry, who took over as executioner in 1883. He calculated that an 11-stone man needed a drop of 9 feet, a 12-stone man needed 8 feet 8 inches, while a 14-stone man needed just 8 feet – and adjusted the rope accordingly.

In 1886 a House of Lords committee on executions laid down the procedure, which was used up until the abolition of the death penalty in 1965, although this still allowed some individual initiative. According to the last hangman, Albert Pierrepoint, the positioning of the knot was crucial – it had to force the victim's head back sharply as they fell, both breaking the neck and rupturing the jugular vein so that death came instantaneously.

Some victims preferred the short-drop method as it offered some hope of salvation. In 1705 John Smith was hanged for housebreaking, but after he had been dangling for 15 minutes, the order came for his reprieve. He was cut down, revived and became famous as 'Half-hanged' Smith.

Another victim was not so lucky. In 1752, doctors in Newcastle-upon-Tyne found a hanged murderer called Macdonald sitting up in the dissecting room. According to one account: 'He immediately begged for mercy; but a young surgeon, not wishing to be disappointed of the dissection, seized a wooden mall, with which he deprived him of his life.'

The pirate Captain Kidd did not have much luck either. When he was hanged at Execution Dock in Wapping on 23

May 1701, the rope broke. Rather than release him, the hangman got another rope and strung him up for a second time. Being a heavy man, he died quickly; his body was cut down, laid on the beach and left for the tide to wash over him three times. Then it was painted in tar, bound in chains and put in a metal harness that would keep his skeleton intact while his flesh rotted away. Finally the body was displayed hanging from a gibbet that cost £10 to build at Tilbury Point, where anyone sailing in or out of the Thames could see it.

Earliest escape

One of the earliest cases where a condemned person survived the hangman in England was that of Inetta de Balsham, who was sentenced to death during the reign of King Henry III for harbouring thieves. She was hanged at 9.00 a.m. on Monday and continued to dangle until the following Thursday when she was found to be still alive. Apparently de Balsham's windpipe was deformed and had become so ossified that the rope failed to stop her breathing. King Henry was so amazed by her survival that he gave her a pardon.

'Take away thy thumb'

Sixteenth-century English thief James Filewood tried to escape execution 'by benefit of clergy' with the help of the legal exemption that stated: 'If the accused could prove he could read, so he would be branded on the hand and freed.' Filewood was illiterate, but a friend who could read agreed to whisper the words in his ear. 'Oh Lord,' read the friend, pausing for

Filewood to repeat his words. Unfortunately, Filewood's thumb was covering the next line of the text, so his friend whispered to him to move it. 'Oh Lord, take away thy thumb,' the dim-witted Filewood repeated. The game was up, but the judge was so amused he spared Filewood's life.

Not one to profit from good fortune, Filewood continued his career of theft, was arrested and accused of stealing a watch. Fortunately for Filewood, the stolen article could not be found to be produced as evidence, but the watch had an alarm which sounded from an inside pocket just as he was about to be released. This time there was no loophole – the watch was returned to its owner and Filewood was hanged.

Unreformed

In 1728 Maggie Dickson, of Musselburgh, Scotland was accused of murdering a child. She protested her innocence. However, as she was being unfaithful to her husband who was away at sea, her character counted against her. She was sent to trial in Edinburgh and hanged at Leith. Her friends cut her down and were taking her back to Musselburgh for burial when she revived. After a good night's sleep in an inn in Pepper Mill that night, she was well enough to walk the remaining two miles home the following day.

Rather than try and hang her again, it was decided that, if God wanted her to live, she must be innocent. Besides, hanging had not taught her a lesson. According to a contemporary account, she became mistress of an alehouse and 'lived and died again in profligacy'.

Help from the crowd

Robert Johnston was unlucky. Hanged for highway robbery in Edinburgh in 1818, his drop was so short that his toes were still touching the scaffold. The crowd, horrified by his agony, surged forward and carried him off, but the police managed to recover him. Returned to the scaffold, the hangman did no better the second time and Johnston, an eyewitness said, 'was suspended with his face uncovered, and one of his hands broke loose from the cords with which it should have been tied, and with his fingers convulsively twitching in the noose'. It took him 40 minutes to die.

Babbacombe Lee

In England if a condemned man survived three attempts to hang him, the sentence was automatically commuted to life imprisonment. The most famous case was that of John Henry George Lee – also known as 'Babbacombe' Lee – a footman who was found guilty of murdering his employer, elderly spinster Emma Ann White Keyse, who had been found hacked to death in the burned-out remains of her villa in Babbacombe, South Devon on 15 November 1884. Sentenced to death on 4 February 1885, Lee was sent to Exeter Gaol in Devon where executioner John Bemy failed three times to despatch him. Lee was eventually released in 1907, still protesting his innocence, toured the country as 'The Man They Could Not Hang' and a silent film was made about his life. In 1917 he emigrated to America where he married and lived on until 1933.

Hanged twice for the same offence?

In 1534, a piper named John Baxtendale was convicted at York assizes and sentenced to hang outside Micklegate Bar. The sentence was duly carried out and he was left swinging for three-quarters of an hour, before being cut down, stripped of his clothes and buried under the gallows tree.

That afternoon, a Mr Vavasour of Hazlewood was riding by and spotted a curious heaving of the earth. When he and his servant stopped and began digging they unearthed the piper who was still breathing. Having washed him down, they returned him to York Castle.

At the next assizes, the question arose whether he could be sentenced again once the sheriff had signed the certificate that the prisoner was already dead and buried. When asked for a fresh death warrant, the judge refused it, saying that providence had plainly intervened on behalf of the piper and that it would be impious to ignore it. The piper went on to become a hostler and lived a long and happy life.

A pressing matter

Under the Statute of Westminster of 1275 those who refused to plead or who challenged more than 20 prospective jurors would be starved into submission. But in 1406 peine forte et dure – a form of torture – was introduced. Unless the accused pleaded guilty or not guilty, they were chained to the ground and weights were piled on top of them until they chose to talk or their internal organs burst and they died. This was used so frequently that Newgate had a special yard set aside for pressing.

The wording of the judgement was:

That the prisoner shall be remanded to the place from whence he came, and put in some low, dark room, and that he shall lie without any litter or other thing under him, and without any manner of garment, except something to hide his privy member; that one arm shall be drawn to one quarter of the room with a cord and the other to another, and that his feet shall be used in the same manner; and that as many weights shall be laid upon him as he can bear, and more; that he shall have three morsels of barley bread a day, and that he shall have the water next to the prison, so that it be not current; and that he shall not eat the same day on which he drinks, not drink on the same day on which he eats; and that he shall continue so till he die or answer.

In 1586, Margaret Clitheroe was crushed to death in York when she refused to answer questions about hiding a priest. Elizabeth I had made 'harbouring a Catholic priest' a hanging offence, but Margaret was only trying to protect the priest who would be hanged, drawn and quartered if caught.

In 1712, Thomas Cross and William Spiggot were ordered to be pressed to death at the Old Bailey. On seeing the preparations being made, Cross gave in and pleaded, but Spigot was made of sterner stuff. His sufferings are described in *The Annals of Newgate*:

The chaplain found him lying in the vault upon the bare ground with 350 pounds weight upon his breast, and then prayed by him, and at several times asked him why he would hazard his soul by such obstinate kind of self-murder. But all the answer he made was – 'Pray for me, pray for me!' He sometimes lay silent under the pressure, as if insensible to pain, and then again would fetch his breath very quick and short. Several times he complained that they had laid a cruel weight upon his face, though it was covered with nothing but a thin cloth, which was afterwards removed; yet he still complained of the prodigious weight on his face, which might be caused by the blood being forced up thither, and pressing the veins as violently as if the force had been externally upon his face. When he had remained for half-an-hour under this load, and 50 pounds weight more laid on, being in all 400 pounds, he told those who attended him he would plead. The weights were at once taken off, the cords cut asunder; he was raised by two men, some brandy was put in his mouth to revive him, and he was carried to take his trial.

Peine forte et dure was not used in treason cases as standing mute was considered a guilty plea. Last used in 1741, it was abolished in 1772 and an Act of 1827 said that a 'not guilty' plea was to be recorded for anyone refusing to plead.

CHAPTER FIFTEEN

Silliness in the City

HE KINGS AND QUEENS OF England and Parliament at Westminster have always made special laws for the City of London, while the Lord Mayor and his aldermen delight in making strange laws for themselves. No matter how ludicrous their ordinances, the City authorities still go to great lengths to uphold their traditions.

Freemen of the City of London

One of the oldest surviving traditions is the granting of the freedom of the City of London which is thought dates back to 1237. In medieval times a freeman was someone who was not the property of a feudal lord and had the right to own land and earn money. The charter of their town or city granted freedom to the tradesmen living within its walls, so craftsmen coming to the city were issued a document making them freemen. This would be conferred in a casket which a freeman would carry around with him to prove he had the right to work. Until 1835, anyone who carried on a trade in the City of London had to be a freeman and a member of one of the ancient guilds or livery companies.

There are a number of ancient privileges that come with being a freeman of the City. Freemen have the right to herd sheep over London Bridge, go about the City with a drawn sword and, if convicted of a capital offence, be hung with a silken cord rather than the standard hemp rope, these rights being more of a collective memory than a written law. It is also thought that freemen are allowed to drive geese down Cheapside, though no one has tried this recently. Other rights are said to have included immunity from press-ganging, being able to marry in St Paul's, being buried within the City walls and being drunk and disorderly without fear of arrest.

Today the freedom of the City has no real privileges, but is still taken up by some 1,800 people every year. Before 1996, it was only open to British subjects or Commonwealth citizens over 21 years of age, and of good character, but nowadays people of any nationality may apply. There is also a long tradition of granting women – who become 'free sisters' – the freedom of the City.

Fletchers

The Worshipful Company of Fletchers was set up in the City of London in 1371, when the arrow-makers presented a petition to the Lord Mayor to make their trade separate and distinct from that of the bowyer, or bow-maker. Anyone caught working in both trades was fined £4. The first masters and wardens of the Company were sworn in in 1385, and the company's first ordinances were issued on 16 June 1403.

In 1423 fletchers were forbidden to open their shops on Sundays and 'high feast days'. And in 1471 a law was passed that allowed the authorities to order fletchers, bowyers, stringers and arrowhead-makers who were not freemen of the City to move to other cities, boroughs or towns where there were no arrow or bow-makers 'for the maintenance of artillery and archery'. Even so there was such a shortage of bows and arrows in the kingdom that an Act had to be passed to allow them to be imported. It was illegal to admit women to the guilds but, in the sixteenth century, the fletchers allowed widows to join on the death of their husbands. Eventually even single women were allowed. Even so, the Company informed a Commission in 1887 that 'no women have hitherto been admitted'.

Apothecaries

The Apothecaries Act of 1815 gave the Worshipful Society of Apothecaries the statutory right to conduct examinations and to grant licences to practise medicine throughout England and Wales. It continues to license doctors to this day as a member of the United Examining Board, the only non-university medical licensing board in the UK.

Not only are they non-medical, the Apothecaries used to be plain old grocers, having begun as the Guild of Pepperers, formed in the City in 1180. By 1316, the Pepperers had been joined by the Spicers, and in due course they became wholesalers, dealing with goods *en gros* – hence grocers – and were incorporated as the Worshipful Company of Grocers in 1428.

Although members continued to work in the growing spice trade, by the mid-sixteenth century specialist apothecaries had become the equivalent of today's high-street chemists which brought them into conflict with the College of Physicians who regulated medicine.

For many years London apothecaries who specialised in pharmacy petitioned to secede from the Grocers' Company. Their leader Gideon de Laune, a wealthy and influential Huguenot, was also apothecary to Anne of Denmark, wife of James I of England, who signed the royal charter incorporating the Worshipful Society of Apothecaries on 6 December 1617.

King James explained his decision to the House of Commons in 1624: 'I myself did devise that corporation and do allow it. The grocers who complain of it are but merchants; the mystery of these apothecaries belonging to apothecaries, wherein the grocers are unskilful; and therefor I think it is fitting they should be a corporation of themselves.'

In 1632, the Society acquired the guest house of the Dominican Priory of Blackfriars as their livery hall. It was destroyed in the Great Fire of London, but rebuilt on the same site in 1672. The Society of Apothecaries manufactured and sold medical and pharmaceutical products at the Hall until 1922, and also ran the Chelsea Physic Garden, founded in 1673, only relinquishing control in 1899.

In 1704, the Society won a key legal suit against the Royal College of Physicians, known as the Rose Case. In February 1701, an apothecary named Rose had sent 'boluses, electuaries and juleps' – large round pills, syrups and medicated drinks – to a man named Seale. Rose was prosecuted for 'practising physic' without a licence, in contravention of an Act of Henry VIII who had granted a charter to the College of Physicians in 1518. He was convicted and he appealed, the case going to the House of Lords, who ruled that apothecaries could both dispense and prescribe medicine. The College tried to strike back several times, but bills attempting to reassert their monopoly on doctoring failed and the Apothecaries Act was passed in 1815 to regulate the situation. It allowed apothecaries to practise after five-years' training, as a consequence of which they evolved into today's general practitioners, or GPs.

Garbling spices

In 1707, James I permitted the 'garbling of spices' in the City of London through the City of London (Garbling of Spices and Admission of Brokers) Act which authorised the Lord Mayor and Aldermen to appoint an official garbler whose duties were 'at the request of any person or persons, owner or owners of any spices, drugs or other wares or merchandises garbleable, and not otherwise, [to] garble the same'. The Act repealed the Spices Act of 1603, which described itself as 'An Act for well Garbling of Spices'. 'To garble', in this sense, means to remove impurities by sifting.

The 1707 Act was repealed by the Food and Drugs Act of 1938. However, Clause 14 of the City of London Elections Act of 1724, which is still in force, allows the City to appoint, rather than elect, the 'coroner, common cryer, commissioners of sewer and garbler'.

Bakers

The Bakers' Guild had the task of enforcing the 'Bread Assize' within two miles of the City of London, excluding the City of Westminster. The assize was maintained by the Court of Halimot or Holy-Moot – 'moot' is an old word for a court – which sat in the guild's hall with a jury formed of the wardens and aldermen and a pair of scales to detect short weights. It also kept an eye out for bakers who put sand or sawdust in the flour – a common practice of the time.

The penalty for a serious offence was to be dragged through the dirtiest streets of the City on a hurdle with an offending loaf hung around the neck; a second offence would earn an hour in the pillory, and if convicted a third time, a baker would have his oven demolished and be forced to foreswear baking. He would certainly not have been able to continue in business in the City as the Bakers' Company issued annual hallmarks – similar to those used on precious metal – for certified bakers to mark their loaves.

Bakers were so fearful of giving short weight that they would give a small extra piece of bread with each loaf. Indeed, with an order of 12 loaves, they would give one loaf free, hence a 'baker's dozen'.

The situation became more complicated in 1572 when the Brown Bakers, who made their loaves using rye, barley or buckwheat, split from the White Bakers to former their own company, but in 1645, due to a decline in trade, they were forced to reunite. The Bread Assize ended in 1815, after which the weight of a standard loaf was fixed by statute.

Fishmongers

Until the end of the fourteenth century the Fishmongers also had their own court of law called the Leyhalmode, where all disputes relating to fish were judged by the wardens. The Weavers also had a court.

Basket-makers

It may well be illegal to sell baskets in the City of London. Until the reign of Edward III, only freemen were allowed to do this, their right being asserted by a number of Acts of Parliament, but Edward allowed a number of foreign basket-makers to settle in the City.

Edward IV tried to restrict the trade again, limiting the number of apprentices and, by an Order of Council dated 1463, basket-makers were confined to Blanche Appleton, a district set aside for aliens in the parish of St Katherine Coleman in Aldgate Ward, near the present Mark Lane.

By the end of the fifteenth century basket-makers had moved out into the parishes of St Andrews and St Margaret Pattens – old vestry books there list gifts or payments they made to the Church. But by this time Blanche Appleton was inundated with foreigners who were importing baskets illegally from Holland, thereby forcing prices down. In the 'Evil May Day' riot of 1517, London apprentices took out their grievances on the foreigners, smashing their windows and breaking down their doors. The Lord Mayor and Aldermen managed to quell the riot, but not until ten pairs of gallows were erected around the City, one in Blanche Appleton.

Then in 1538, a fire broke out on the basket-makers' premises in the parish of St Margaret Pattens, more than a dozen houses were burned down and nine people died. As a result basket-makers were ordered to leave the City and although they fought the order, which was suspended until 1541, Henry VIII confirmed their expulsion.

There is no record of the expulsion order being repealed, but City records show that basket-makers had returned by 1565. Following the restoration of the monarchy in 1660, the basket-makers tried to regularise their situation by applying for a charter from the Crown to incorporate as a City livery company, having previously obtained their freedom by joining the Butchers' and Turners' Companies', two trades that used a lot of baskets. But their applications to form their own company were turned down in 1682, 1685 and 1698, and it was only in 1937 that the basket-makers were finally granted a royal charter by George VI. To this day no one knows whether they are really allowed to reside or sell their wares within the City.

Silk-throwers

The 1662 Silk Throwing Act establishing the City of London's Company of Silk-throwers said that people who 'unjustly, deceitfully and salsly purloined, imbezilled, pawned, sold or detained' silk and made no recompense for the loss would be subject to punishment by whipping or being put in the stocks.

Beards and breeches

In the reign of Henry VIII, the Court of Aldermen of the City of London took out an order against 'persons with great beards'. They were also told to 'have a vigilant eye to all the inhabitants of their wards etc using to wear outrageous breeches, etc in their apparel and to commit transgressors therein'.

The rules and regulations had become even stricter by 1611. An Act of Common Council was passed 'for reformation of apparel to be worn by apprentices, and maid-servants within the City of London, and the liberties thereof'. It specified that no apprentice could wear 'any hat lined, faced or turfed with velvet, silk or taffata … nor any hat, other than such, as the hat and band with trimming, shall not exceed in all, the value or price of five shillings'. Neither was he to wear bands in expensive materials such as lawn or cambric, but 'holland or other linen, not exceeding the price or value of five shillings'. They were not to be edged with lace or any other work, but should have a plain hem with only one stitch. The material in ruff-bands was not to exceed three yards in length before they were gathered, and not to be more than two inches in depths before they were set in the stock.

In addition, 'no apprentice shall wear any Pickadilly' – an ornate raised collar – 'or other support, in, with, or about the collar of his doublet, nor shall wear about his collar, either point, ribbon or lace'. Instead, collars were to be made of cloth. Doublets and breeches were not to be made out of 'any kind of silk, or stuff mingled with silk, but only of cloth, kersey, fustian, sackcloth, canvas, English leather or English stuff, which stuff shall not exceed the price or value of two shillings and six pence a yard'.

An apprentice's cloak, coat, jerkin, doublet or breeches could not be made of any broadcloth worth more than 10s 0d a yard, or kersey worth more than 5s 0d a yard. 'Garnishing, lining, facing' and the like were not to be made of velvet or silk, though silk buttons and buttonholes were allowed. He was not allowed to wear gloves worth more than 12d a pair, and fringing or garnishing with 'gold or silver, lace, velvet, silk, or silk lace, or ribbon' was banned. Also banned were any 'girdle, point, garters or shoestrings of any kind of silk or ribbon, nor any rose or such like toys at all, either on his garters or his shoes'.

After the feast day of St Michael the Archangel, apprentices were not to wear 'any silk, worsted or jersey stockings'. Woollen yarn or kersey alone were not allowed, nor could they 'wear any Spanish-leather shoes, nor any shoes made with Polonia [Polish] heels, nor any shoes made of any other leather than neat's [ox] leather or calves leather'. And their hair was to be worn without 'any tuft or lock, but cut in decent and comely manner'.

For a first offence, the apprentice would receive a simple rebuke from his master; for a second offence, the apprentice was to be brought before the chamberlain of the City and locked up for at least 18 hours and fined 3s 4d, half going to the poor of the parish and half to the person who informed on him.

Fashion and farthingales

Women's fashions was also causing the City fathers distress, so the 1611 Act sought to avoid the 'many and great inconveniences and disorders which daily grow, by the inordinate pride of maid-servant and women servants in their excess of apparel and folly in variety of new fashions'.

Consequently no maiden servant or woman servant living or working in the City of London shall 'wear up her head any lawne, cambric, tiffiny, cobweb-lawne or white silk-cipres, either in any kerchief, coif, cross-cloth or shadow, nor any linen cloth therein, saving such linen cloth only, which shall not exceed the price or value of five shillings the eln [forty-five inches]'. Lace and edging was banned, while 'bands, neckerchiefs, strippes or stomachers' all had to be plain, and ruffs could not be longer that four yards before gathering, or deeper than three inches.

Lawn, cambric, tiffiny, cobweb-lawn, white silk-cipres or linen cloth worth more than 5s od an eln were banned. Lacing and edging were also out and only a plain hem with one stitch was allowed. Also banned was 'any stomacher wrought with any gold, silver or silk or with any kind of stuff made of silk or mixed with silk'.

It was also against the law to hire a female servant wearing 'any gown, kirtle, waistcoat or petticoat, old or new, of any kind of silk stuff, or stuff mingled with silk, or any other stuff exceeding the price of two shillings and five pence a yard; nor any kersey exceeding the price of five shillings a yard; nor broadcloth exceeding the price of ten shillings a yard'. She was not to wear 'any silk lace or guard upon her gown, kirtle, waistcoat or petticoat, or any other garment, save only a cape of velvet'.

Farthingales – hoops worn to expand the hipline – were completely out and women were not allowed wire or whalebone stiffeners in bodices and sleeves, only canvas and buckram. Silk, lawn and cambric were banned in aprons, along with any material that cost more than 2s 6d a yard. An apron was not allowed to be more than 'one breadth' of material wide nor to have any edging, lace or fringing on it. Worsted, jersey and silk stockings were banned along with 'any Spanish-leather shoes, shoes of any other leather, only neat's leather or calves leather; nor any shoes whatsoever with Polonia heels; nor with the same any stitching, rose or like ribbon for shoe-strings'.

For a first offence a woman would be fined 3s 4d and for a second offence, 5s 8d 'or the apparel worn contrary to the true meaning hereof'. Again half the fine would go to the poor of the parish and half to the informer – if the offender did not pay up, they would be prosecuted for debt.

This Act was made law in 1611 – and the Corporation of London does not know whether it is still in force.

Tower of London

By law, every Royal Navy ship that visits the port of London must deliver a barrel of rum to the Constable of the Tower of the London. The rum was delivered in lieu of the portion of cargo that the Constable got, from the fourteenth century onwards, from other vessels that moored under the protection of his guns.

As it is rare these days for a ship of the Royal Navy to steam into the port of London, the tradition is maintained annually with the ceremony of the Constable's Dues. Once a year the Royal Navy moors one of its ships alongside the Tower Pier and the captain delivers a barrel of rum to the Constable as a symbol of these ancient rights. The captain and his escort of naval ratings, flanked by a contingent of Yeoman Warders in state dress, and a corps of drum, march through the Tower to Tower Green where the barrel is handed over. Afterwards the participants retire to the Queen's House – the Constable's – to sample the contents.

Another of the Constable's perks was revenue from any horses, oxen, pigs or sheep that fell off London Bridge or any cart that fell into the moat. Owners recovering livestock from the moat had to pay a penny a foot – which usually worked out at 4d an animal. And all vegetation growing on Tower Hill belonged to the Constable.

The Constable was also entitled to demand 6s 8d a year from the owners of all boats fishing for sprat between the Tower and the sea, a shilling a year from all ships carrying herring to London and 2d from each pilgrim who came to London by sea to worship at the shrine of St James.

The Tower Liberties

The Tower and the surrounding area known as the 'Tower Liberties' is independent of the City and outside the jurisdiction of both the Lord Mayor and the Bishop of London. In the fourteenth century the location of the boundary markers was impressed on the minds of the local boys by giving them a severe thrashing. These days the ceremony of the 'beating of the bounds' is not so savage. It takes place on Ascension Day every three years when local children, armed with willow wands, beat the boundary stones.

Ravens

Under a decree of Charles II six ravens must be kept in the Tower at all times. According to legend, if the ravens leave, both the Tower and the Kingdom will fall. Although their wings are clipped to prevent them flying away, some ravens

have escaped – others have been dismissed for bad behaviour. As insurance the Raven Master keeps chicks on site in hatcheries to replace any that go missing.

Bum-boats

In 1762 the delightfully named Bum-boat Act was passed. Bum-boats were originally boats permitted under Trinity House Bye Laws of 1685 to removed the 'filth' from ships lying at anchor in the Thames. But they soon began selling fruit, vegetables and other provisions to the ships. The 1762 Act aimed to regulate this trade, which must have been unsavoury if not unhygienic. Bum-boats had to be registered and numbered.

City of London scam

In 1748, the City of London came up with a wonderful money-making scam – it passed a bye-law that imposed a fine of £600 on any 'able and fit person' who, after being nominated as a City officer, refused to serve.

Under the Corporation Act of 1661 all city officials were required to swear an oath and take the sacrament under the rites of the Church of England. So the City fathers set about nominating a series of nonconformists as sheriff, who, as dissenters, would refuse the sacrament. Consequently, they could not take office and would have to pay the fine.

Eventually a dissenter named Evans took the matter to the House of Lords who found the practice illegal under the Toleration Act of 1689, which allowed nonconformists to worship as they chose. But in the six years the bye-law was in force, the

City of London raised £15,000 – enough to build its new Mansion House.

London rents

Every year, the solicitor to the City of London pays for a piece of land that the Corporation rented in Shropshire over 700 years ago – even though the location of this land has long been forgotten and the rent is just one blunt billhook and one sharp axe.

The rent is paid every October in a bizarre ritual called the Quit-Rents Ceremony in which the City Solicitor, resplendent in his black gown, must try and cut through a bundle of wood with the billhook, and fail; then he must succeed in cutting through a similar bundle with the axe. Finally the tools and bundles are presented to an officer of the Crown known as the Queen's Remembrancer.

The City must also stump up 61 nails and six horseshoes for a long-defunct forge in the Strand that had been rented from Henry III in 1235 by a blacksmith named Walter le Brun, when his shoeing shop stood next to the jousting-fields of the Knights Templar near St Clement Danes.

Trial of the Pyx

The Queen's Remembrancer is also responsible for the annual Trial of the Pyx. This is the trial of weight and quality of the coins produced that year by the Royal Mint, which has been carried out since 1248 and has been confirmed by a series of Coinage Acts down the ages, the most recent being the Coinage Act of 1971.

In the course of the year, the Royal Mint puts aside one coin out of every 5,000 minted worth more than ten pence and one out of every 20,000 coins worth ten pence or less. These are stored in a pyx, a cylindrical box with a lid. Each February the Queen's Remembrancer and a panel of six jurymen known as the Prince Warden and Wardens, who are freemen of the Worshipful Company of Goldsmiths, meet in Goldsmiths' Hall in full regalia. They check the number and denomination of the coins to see that the right number has been produced, and the weights and diameters of the coins are checked to see if they fall within the correct 'remedy' or tolerance required by law.

The National Weights and Measures Laboratory of the Department of Trade produces the weights for use in the trial and also makes standard 'trial plates' of gold, silver, copper and nickel. These are cut in two in a jagged fashion, one half being supplied to the Royal Mint as a template for them to work to, the other half being used in the trial. The two halves of the trial plate can be fitted back together to prove that they are both working to the same standard and neither the Crown nor the people are being defrauded.

The coins are then assayed against pieces of metal cut from these trial plates to make sure that the fineness or composition and purity of the metal used is correct. Although gold and silver coins no longer circulate as currency in Britain, they are still produced for commemorative or ceremonial purposes such as the distribution of Maundy Money. Each year on Maundy Thursday – the Thursday before Easter – in a ceremony that goes back to Edward I, the reigning monarch hands out a set of silver coins to a number of people equal to the sovereign's age.

The actual measuring and testing of coins is done at the London Assay Office over a period of eight to ten weeks. The Trial of the Pyx reconvenes when the testing is done and the verdict of the jury is delivered each May to the Master of the Mint, or his deputy, and the Queen's Remembrancer, to confirm that the coinage of the realm is sound for another year. According to law:

> The verdict of the jury shall be in writing and signed by each of the jurymen and shall be handed to the Queen's Remembrancer, who shall authenticate it with his signature, deposit it with the records of his office and deliver a copy of it to the Treasury. The Queen's Remembrancer shall direct that the verdict, or those parts of the verdict which he considers appropriate, shall be read aloud in his presence. The Treasury shall deliver one copy of the verdict to the proper officers of the Department of Trade and Industry and another copy to the Deputy Master of the Mint and shall cause the verdict to be published in the *London Gazette*.

Originally the trial was needed to check that the Master of the Mint was not cheating. These days, of course, the weight, size and composition of British coins are checked by machine and computer at the Royal Mint.

Although the verdict of the Trial of the Pyx may seem like a forgone conclusion, in 1710 the jury reported that the coins had fallen below standard, but the then Master of the Mint, Sir Isaac Newton, was able to show that the trial plate of 1707 had been made too fine. He managed to get it withdrawn and the Mint returned to the trial plate of 1688.

After 1837, the old trial plates were stored, along with old coinage dies, in the Pyx Chapel in the cloisters of Westminster Abbey, which dates from the reign of William the Conqueror. The earliest surviving trial plate is a silver ingot dating from 1278 or 1279. The chapel houses a virtually unbroken series of gold and silver trial plates from 1477 onwards, including the disputed 1707 plate. Only a tiny fragment remains of the 1688 trial plate after its reuse.

Burlington Arcade

There is another small enclave with its own jurisdiction, a mile-and-a-half to the west, called Burlington Arcade. It is a covered mall of tiny shops, many with their original signs, that runs for 196 yards between Piccadilly and Old Burlington Street where the laws of the Regency still apply.

The arcade was built in 1818 by Lord George Cavendish, later to become the Earl of Burlington, and designed by architect Samuel Ware 'for the sale of jewellery and fancy articles of fashionable demand, for the gratification of the public'. From the moment the gates were first thrown open in 1819, it was an instant success with the fashionable ladies and dandies of the day.

Nearly two centuries later, Burlington Arcade retains Regency decorum by banning singing, humming, whistling, hurrying and 'behaving boisterously'. The laws are enforced by a corps of Burlington Arcade Beadles, originally recruited by Lord Cavendish from his regiment, the 10th Hussars. Things have moved on though – today the beadles wear Edwardian frock coats, gold buttons and gold-braided top hats. The laws have had to change with the times too – originally it was for-bidden to carry a parcel in the arcade, but today's shoppers would never comply with that.

Top hat

Who would have thought that Fred Astaire could have been considered an incorrigible law-breaker? But when he was put-ting on his top hat, tying up his white tie and brushing off his tails, he was breaking the law – in England at least.

The precedent was set in 1797 when the inventor of the top hat, London haberdasher John Hetherington, deciding to give his new hat its public debut, left his shop in the Strand and went for a drive through the City. The sight of his hat caused a sensation, people booed, several women fainted, a crowd gathered and a small boy got his arm broken in the crush.

Hetherington was arrested, arraigned before the Lord Mayor of London and charged with conduct likely to cause a breach of the King's peace, in particular: 'appearing on the public highway wearing upon his head a tall structure having a shining lustre and calculated to frighten timid people'. Found guilty he was fined £50, an enormous sum in those days.

Metropolitan Police Act

A great many house-proud Londoners must unwittingly be breaking the law every day. Under section 60, Paragraph 3 of the catch-all Metropolitan Police Act of 1839, it is an offence to 'beat or shake any carpet, rug or mat in any street in the

Metropolitan Police District' – the penalty being a fine of £2 – although it is permitted to shake out a doormat, as long as you do it before eight o'clock in the morning. The same paragraph also bans waste from slaughterhouses and hanging beds out of windows.

The next paragraph imposes a similar fine on:

> every person who shall empty or begin to empty a privy between the hours of six in the morning and twelve at night, or remove along any thoroughfare any night soil, soap lees, ammoniacal liquor or other such offensive matter, between the hours of six in the morning and eight in the evening, or who shall at any time use for any such purpose any cart or carriage not having a proper covering, or who shall carelessly slop or spill any such offensive matter … this enactment shall not be construed to prevent the commissioner of any sewers within the Metropolitan Police District, or any person acting in the service or by their direction, from emptying or removing along any thoroughfare at any time the contents of any sewer which they are authorised to cleanse or empty.

And Londoners are not allowed to keep a pigsty in the front of their houses. This section is still in force, but the section preventing you heating or melting 'pitch, fat, rosin, grease, tallow, oil or other combustible matter' on board ship between Westminster Bridge and Blackwall has been repealed.

You are not allowed to 'blow any horn' unless you are a guard or a postman belonging to Her Majesty's postal service in the performance of your duty. And £2 and up to seven days in gaol is still the punishment for drunkards guilty of riotous or indecent behaviour. Nor are you allowed to 'sing any profane, indecent or obscene song or ballad, or write or draw any indecent or obscene word, figure or representation, or use any profane, indecent or obscene language'.

The slaughtering or dressing of cattle in the streets is still illegal, except if the animal concerned has been run over by the person who is doing the slaughtering or dressing; it is forbidden under the Metropolitan Streets Act of 1867 to drive cattle down the roadway between 10.00 a.m. and 7.00 p.m. without prior approval from the Commissioner of Police; and it is unlawful for anyone who 'lives within a mile of any arsenal or store for explosives' to possess a pack of playing cards.

CHAPTER SIXTEEN

Provincial Peccadilloes

 LTHOUGH LONDON HAS a great many strange laws, there are plenty in the provinces too. While no one seems worried about dress codes here, sex and general naughtiness are a concern all over.

Welshmen in Chester

After the rebellion of Owen Glendower in Wales in 1403, the Earl of Chester – the future Henry V – ordered that all Welsh people and Welsh sympathisers should be expelled from the city. The city ordinance also states: 'No Welshman may enter the city before sunrise or stay after sunset on pain of decapitation.'

There is a similar piece of folklore about Hereford where, it is said, you can shoot a Welsh person at any time of the day on a Sunday provided you do it with a longbow in the Cathedral Close. And in York, it is said, it is perfectly legal to shoot a Scotsman with a bow and arrow, except on Sundays.

In fact, the people of Chester were far from harsh on

Welshmen – Chester is, after all, a border town. Records show that many stood surety for Welshmen arrested under the order and there is no reference to anyone ever paying the maximum penalty for this crime. The perceived Welsh threat continued throughout the fifteenth century and there is no record that Henry V's order was ever repealed; the result is the belief that any Welsh person could still be shot within the city walls after dark!

A lot of anti-Celtic feeling seems to have been centred on Chester. Under a law of the interregnum passed on 1 October 1646, Irishmen who had been granted the freedom of the city of Chester were to be disenfranchised.

Congleton

Nearby Congleton is not to be outdone. According to Congleton Borough Council, there are local bye-laws against indecent bathing, loitering at church doors and carrying soot:

> No person shall within two hundred yards of any street or public place, unless effectually screened from view, bathe from the bank or strand of any water, or from any boat thereon, without wearing a dress or covering sufficient to prevent indecent exposure of the person. No person shall wilfully and persistently loiter at or near the entrance to any church, chapel or other place of public worship to the annoyance or obstruction of any persons going to, attending at or returning from divine service in such church, chapel or other place of public worship. No person shall in any street or public place, to the inconvenience or danger

of passengers, carry or convey along any footpath any bag of soot, lime or other offensive substance, or any pointed or edged tools or implements not properly protected.

These bye-laws are still in force.

Street-walking in Cambridge

On 26 April 1561, Elizabeth I issued a Charter giving the University of Cambridge jurisdiction over the town. This was confirmed by statute in 1591, which gave Oxford University similar jurisdiction over Oxford for the 'suppressing of vice'. Although this Act is still in force today, it faced an interesting challenge in the 1890s.

One night a young lady by the name of Daisy Hopkins was arrested by the university constables and charged by one of the Pro-Proctors with 'walking with a member of the university in a public street of the town of Cambridge and within the precincts of the university'. Not that there was anything wrong with walking – the university was simply trying to stop its members consorting with women of the night, only it was too polite to say so. According to a learned judge, for many years it had been the practice 'instead of putting down the actual delinquencies against these women – and I suppose many of them have been convicted – in mercy to these women they do not keep a record of the actual facts, but they have put down for years and years, "walking with a member of the university".'

Miss Hopkins appeared the next day before the Vice-Chancellor's Court, was duly convicted and the Vice-Chancellor sentenced her to fourteen days in the 'spinning house or house of correction in the university and town of Cambridge'. But Daisy was not going to take this lying down, applied for a writ of habeas corpus and was granted it. The court found the conviction could not be upheld as it was based on a charge couched in terms that did not specify anything that was an offence, even though everyone – including, presumably, the accused – knew what the real offence was supposed to be.

The Chief Justice, Lord Coleridge said: 'Nobody would suppose that a person simply walking with a member of the university, who might be that member's mother, or sister, or wife, or friend, was guilty of an offence against the law which would justify the Vice-Chancellor in imprisoning him or her.' The language the charge had been framed in – through Victorian modesty or misplaced chivalry – made it impossible for the conviction to stand.

But having beaten the university so decisively, Daisy became overconfident and sued the Pro-Proctor for damages for wrongful imprisonment. This time the courts found that she was pushing her luck and the suit failed.

Gibbet law

The Halifax Gibbet – also known at the Halifax 'Maiden' – was an early guillotine used for public executions between the thirteenth and seventeenth centuries. It was built in 1286 and it is thought that it was first used to punish those who stole cloth from tenters, the wooden frames on which local cloth was stretched and dried. The mechanism was so heavy that it had to be raised by the crowd with all the spectators pulling together. Once raised, the blade would be secured with a pin. When this was pulled out, according to the chronicler Hollinshed, the blade fell with such force 'that if the neck of the transgressor were so big as that of a bull, it should be cut in sunder at a stroke, and roll from the body a huge distance'.

The accused would be presented to the Lord Bailiff by one of the four frith-burghers and the trial would take place before a jury. If found guilty the culprit would be executed immediately if it was market day. Otherwise they would be held in the stocks with the stolen goods on their back until the next market day. If the transgressor had been convicted of stealing cattle, the animal itself would be allowed to act as the executioner and pull the pin.

However, the gibbet laws gave the convicted criminal a second chance – if they were quick enough to pull their head out after the blade was released and flee out of town, they would be free. On 29 January 1623, one John Lacy did just that, but after seven years he grew homesick. However, when he arrived back in Halifax, he was re-arrested and taken back to the gibbet, but the intervening years had slowed him down and the second time he was not so lucky.

Between 1541 and 1650, 53 people are known to have been beheaded on the gibbet, which originally stood on Cow Green, but was later moved to Gibbet Street. After it was taken out of commission in 1650 the actual site was lost; however it was rediscovered by workmen in 1839, along with two skeletons, thought to be the gibbet's last victims. In all eight decapitated remains were found on the site.

Rural rumours

In Great Yarmouth there is an ordinance banning the naming of streets after Shakespeare, Chaucer, Milton, Bryon, Tennyson or any other great poet. A spokesman for the town council is quoted as saying: 'In our opinion, the moral character of these people is not such that we should name roads after them.'

In Kidderminster, it is an offence to own a bath without a watertight plug, while in Upton-upon-Severn it is illegal for married couples to live in a discarded bus. And in Biddenden, Kent, cockerels are not allowed to crow to greet the dawn unless they are more than 200 yards from any place of human habitation.

Newmarket sickness

In Newmarket it was against the law to blow your nose in the street and 'a person or persons going about the street with a head cold or distemper' was liable to a fine. The reason for this was not to protect the human citizens of Newmarket – it was designed to protect the numerous valuable horses that are trained in the town.

Digging for bait

There is an ancient law dating from 1171 that forbids digging worms for bait in a number of coastal areas. In 1993, one early-morning digger was caught in the act at the mouth of the River Blackwater near Maldon, Essex, fined £50 and warned that he risked a fine of £1,000 if caught again. The local river bailiff said that he enforced the ancient law because anti-fouling paint on the hulls of the bait-diggers' boats was doing serious damage to the nearby oyster beds.

Stocks in Broadstairs

Ladies are not allowed to show their ankles in public in St Peters, the original fishing and smuggling village from which Broadstairs in Kent grew. It was one of the very many offences for which you could be put in the village stocks.

Mindful of the 1405 Act instructing every parish to have a set of stocks, Thanet District Council re-installed stocks in Broadstairs a few years ago – though, it has to be said, largely as a tourist attraction rather than as a serious deterrent to crime or flagrant ankle-flashing.

Exclusion

Conwy's city charter states that no Jew might dwell in the borough at any time, just like Catholics were banned from the City of London and Westminster in 1688 and were not given their full civil liberties until the Religious Disabilities Act of 1846.

There are still some national restrictions on Jews and Catholics. Under the Jews Relief Act of 1858, if a 'person professing the Jewish Religion' becomes prime minister, they are not allowed to advise on the appointment of any ecclesiastical post in the Churches of England, Ireland or Scotland – the duties are to devolve on the Archbishop of Canterbury. This Act was passed at a time when Benjamin Disraeli, who became Britain's first Jewish prime minister in 1868, was Chancellor of the Exchequer. The Act apes the Roman Catholic Relief Act of 1829, which excuses Catholics from the same duties – although no such act prohibits a prime minister who is a nonconformist, a Muslim, a Hindu, a Sikh, a Buddhist or even an atheist picking the next Archbishop of Canterbury.

Gypsies

Gypsies have been a feature of the English countryside, on and off, since the sixteenth century. In 1519, the Earl of Surrey entertained 'Gypsions' at Tendring Hall, Suffolk, and gave them safe conduct. But they soon fell out of favour with the authorities and the Egyptians Act of 1530 – gypsies were then thought to have come from Egypt – banned immigration and required all gypsies to leave the country 'voluntarily' within 16 days. The punishment for those who did not conform was the confiscation of goods and property, imprisonment and deportation.

This law was amended in 1554 which then stated that if gypsies abandoned their 'naughty, idle and ungodly life and company' and adopted a sedentary way of life with a settled occupation, they would not be punished – although the punishment was extended to include execution for those not complying. Even though such executions stopped in the latter half of the seventeenth century, the punitive and restrictive laws continued with Romany girls being flogged for filching and fortune-telling.

Attitudes changed when, in January 1753, an 18-year-old serving girl, Elizabeth Canning, went missing for four weeks. When she returned, she claimed she had been abducted by gypsies who had tried to 'induce her to adopt an immoral life'. Six gypsies were arrested and appeared at the Old Bailey before Henry Fielding, the novelist. Despite conflicting evidence, one gypsy woman was condemned to be burned on the hand, another hanged. But the Lord Mayor, Sir Christopher Gascoyne, was convinced that a miscarriage of justice had been done and pardoned them; Elizabeth Canning was later convicted of perjury and transported.

Ten years later the Egyptian Act was repealed because of its 'excessive severity', but those who practised palmistry and fortune-telling were deemed rogues and vagabonds in 1743 and liable to three months' imprisonment.

Things were little better north of the border. As early as 1449, the Scottish Parliament took against 'sorners [spongers], overliers [beggars who did not pay for their lodgings] and masterful beggars with horse, hounds or other goods'. In 1587 James VI promised to take action against 'the wicked and counterfeit thieves and limmers [scoundrels or prostitutes] calling themselves Egyptians'.

In 1603, a special 'Act anent [concerning] the Egiptians' made it 'lesome' to put to death any gypsy – man, woman or child – remaining in Scotland. Moses Faa appealed against the Act as a loyal subject in 1609 and gained the protection of David, Earl of Crawford, but two years later, four Faas were tried in Edinburgh under the anti-gypsy Acts, convicted and executed the same day. Eight gypsies were executed on Burgh Muir in 1624 and their women and children exiled. More were hanged at Haddington in 1636 and their women drowned. Women who had children were to be scourged and branded on the face.

CHAPTER SEVENTEEN

It Doesn't Add Up

 HERE ARE A GREAT MANY STRANGE laws about weights and measures, taxes, money, markets and days of the week that just do not seem to add up.

Thieves' market

For over 800 years, England's numerous outdoor markets were run under the so-called 'Thieves Charter' which was introduced in 1189 and officially known as the 'Market Overt Rules'. An early form of consumer protection, they maintained that anything bought from a stallholder between sunrise and sunset was the legal property of the buyer – even if it turned out that it had been stolen. For centuries markets flourished because these rules exempted purchasers from the usual laws governing stolen property and gave the original owner no redress. Market Overt Rules were abolished by Act of Parliament in January 1995, but outdoor antique markets still manage to survive.

A hole in the law

A street trader who was repeatedly prosecuted for selling doughnuts at Market Cross in Chichester, Sussex, sought the protection of a 500-year-old edict by the Bishop of Chichester which he had come across in the local library. When the bishop had sold Market Cross in 1501, he had recorded in the deed that 'peasants should be free to sell goods there without let or hindrance from the mayor or established traders'. However, when the case reached the Court of Appeal in 1994, the justices ruled that it had been superseded by a ban on street traders passed in 1807.

Window tax

The House and Window Duties Act of 1766 imposed an annual tax of 3s 0d – 15p – on every house in England and 1s 0d – 5p – on every house in Scotland, though houses in Scotland with not more than five windows were exempt.

To make the tax progressive, an extra tax was imposed on windows. For houses with 7 windows, a tax of 2d a window was to be paid; 8 windows attracted 6d a window; 9 windows, 8d a window; 10 windows, 10d a window; 11 windows, a shilling

a window and so on up to 25 windows which attracted a yearly sum of 2s od for every window.

The result? Homeowners bricked up unwanted windows, some of which can still be seen today.

Coal tax

Under the Local Coal and Wine Duties Continuance Act of 1861, some 260 coal posts, or more properly coal and wine tax posts, were erected 15 miles outside the City of London. These were the points at which canals, other navigable waterways, public roads and railways first entered the Metropolitan Area, and it was there that duty became payable on coal and wine coming into the City.

The Corporation of London had exercised the right of 'metage' on coal and other commodities since medieval times, and these rights were confirmed by two charters issued by James I, allowing the city to set up 'a boundary stone, or some other permanent mark' where any turnpike entered the City. The taxes levied were used to rebuild St Paul's Cathedral, numerous other City churches, the Guildhall, the City's markets and Newgate Prison after the Great Fire of London.

A further Act was passed in 1694 'for the Relief of the Orphans and Other Creditors of the City of London'. This gave the City the power to impose a duty on each tun (a large cask) of wine entering the Port of London and increase the duty payable on coal. Once all debts for rebuilding the City had been repaid, surplus funds were used to finance public works including building bridges over the Thames, paving the streets and constructing new access roads into London.

Until the nineteenth century, the transport of coal and other goods into London had been by sea. But the growth of the canal and railway systems meant that collecting points for taxes had to be set up beyond the boundary of the City, so posts were erected on streams, cart tracks and footpaths. The revenue raised was used for metropolitan improvement schemes including the building of the Thames Embankment, the erection of the Holborn Viaduct and the purchase of some private Thames bridges to free them from tolls.

The tax was abolished by an Act of Parliament in 1889, but many posts remained and are now protected as Grade II listed structures. They come in different shapes and sizes, most being cast-iron bollards about 1.2 metres high, erected after the 1861 Act. These are normally to be found by the sides of roads, but can be seen in open countryside too, by tracks and on boundary lines. There are also granite obelisks around 1.2 metres high, erected on the banks of canals and rivers, and cast-iron boxes or plates, about 230 mm square, built into parapets of bridges. Cast-iron or stone obelisks, just under 4.5 metres high, were built by the sides of railways prior to the 1861 Act, while after the Act small 1.5-metre cast-iron obelisks were erected beside the tracks.

Of the original 250–260 posts 219 have survived in some form, though some have been moved to new positions.

Impersonating a Chelsea Pensioner

It is illegal to impersonate a Chelsea Pensioner. It is generally thought that this law was enacted to prevent conmen stealing the pensions of these old gentlemen, some of whom were not so innocent. The Chelsea and Kilmainham Hospitals Act of 1826, which offers this protection, also allows the hospital commissioners to discharge any pensioner 'convicted of a felony or misdemeanour, or who shall in any way misconduct himself'. Kilmainham Hospital was the Irish equivalent of the Chelsea Hospital when England and Ireland were still united.

Plainly both hospitals had trouble with some old rascals at the time. Another provision of the Act required all linen at the veterans' home to be stamped with the name of the hospital to stop the pensioners stealing the sheets. The Act made it specifically illegal for 'any pensioner or other person or persons [to] unlawfully pawn, sell, embezzle, secrete or dispose of, or for any pawnbroker or other person or persons [to] unlawfully take in pawn, buy, exchange or received any clothes, linen, stores or other goods or articles marked, stamped or branded as aforesaid'. This law is still in force.

Pennies and farthings

The Fine Arts Copyright Act of 1862 sought to prevent the making or circulation of copies of pictures that were still in copyright, providing that 'for every such offence' the offender was to pay the copyright holder 'a sum not exceeding £10'. This seemed reasonable enough, if a hundred or even a thousand copies had been circulated, but what happened if a copyright picture was printed in a newspaper where the circulation might run into millions? Even if the smallest damages were levied for a single offence the total would be astronomical.

In 1899, in a case involving a publication with a circulation of a quarter of a million, the Court of Appeal in Ireland decided that each single offence must at least carry a penalty of the smallest amount in circulation, which was then a farthing – a quarter of an old penny or just over 0.1p. An English court followed suit in 1901 in a case that involved a paper with a circulation of a million. On appeal, the newspaper argued that the Mint had once produced coins smaller than a farthing – half farthings and even mites, which were a sixth of an old penny.

The Court of Appeal cleared up the matter by deciding that a single penalty could be levied for multiple of offences that did not have to be exactly divisible by the number of offences – in fact, the principle had been established by two cases in the seventeenth century. In 1618, a jury awarded half-a-farthing damages for trespass, even though no such coin existed at that time. In Oxford you could get a draft of beer for half-a-farthing, which meant you would have had to buy more than one at a time.

Nude pact

Under English Common Law, if you are owed £1, you cannot accept 95p in settlement. According to the Master of the Rolls in 1881, Mr Justice Kessel: 'A creditor can accept anything to settle a debt, except for a lesser amount of money. He might take a horse, or a canary, or a tomtit if he chose, and that was accord and satisfaction; but, by an most extraordinary peculiarity of English Common Law, he could not take 19s 6d in the pound; that was *nudum pactum*.'

Nudum pactum means 'nude pact', which means a one-sided contract, written or verbal, that is not clothed in the consideration required by law. English law requires that both parties to a contract benefit to some degree, so a nude pact is invalid. Kessel's judgement continued: 'Although the creditor might take a canary, yet, if the debtor did not give him a canary together with his 19s 6d, there is no accord and satisfaction; if he did, there was accord and satisfaction. That is one of the mysteries of English Common Law.' Surprisingly, under Scottish law, nude pacts are allowed.

The cost of inflation

In 1923, a gentleman named Franklin paid a cheque for 9,000 million marks into Westminster Bank. It was drawn on a bank in Berlin, when Germany was undergoing runaway inflation, and he was credited £15 for it. The Westminster Bank lost out too. By the time they presented the cheque, Germany had revalued, issuing one new mark for every one million million of the old ones. The cheque was now worth nine thousandths of a new mark, less than a tenth of a penny, a transaction so small that the bank could not even be bothered with it. However, in 1929 Mr Franklin sued Westminster Bank for £459,000,000, claiming that the cheque was worth its face value in new marks. After a day in court, the judge dismissed the case as 'absurd and ridiculous'.

The invisible bonds

In 1939, a wealthy Austrian who had some bearer bonds drawn on the Bank of England wanted to get them out of his country, which had just been taken over by the Nazis. He dare not risk sending them by mail or by courier in case they were intercepted, so instead he arranged for two English solicitors to meet him in a hotel room in Vienna where he showed them the bonds and told them to take careful note of the value and numbers.

Once they had done that, he asked them to watch carefully as he went over to the fireplace and burned the bonds one by one. He then asked them to return to London and tell the Bank of England what they had seen.

Back in London the two solicitors made a statutory declaration that the bonds had been destroyed and the Bank issued a new set to replace them. These remained outside Austria and were available whenever the wealthy Austrian needed them.

Law's a lottery

One of the niceties of the Commonwealth is that plaintiffs in distant lands still have the right of appeal to the Judicial Committee of the Privy Council. In 1931, a case was brought from Trinidad, then still a colony, concerning a local lottery that was decided by spinning four discs in row, each bearing the numbers zero to nine. When the winning number 9351 came up, it was disputed by holder of ticket number 1539, who asserted that the numbers should be read off in the usual way from left to right, not right to left, the way the lottery organisers has read them. The Supreme Court of Trinidad and Tobago agreed with him, but their decision was reversed by the Privy Council on the grounds that the lottery tickets carried a condition obliging all ticket holders to abide by the decision of the stewards of the club organising the lottery.

Making a deposit

You can be fined and risk going to gaol for making a deposit at your bank – if that deposit is dung. Farmer David Cannon made repeated deposits of steaming manure at NatWest's Ponteland and Newcastle-upon-Tyne branches, bespattering the banks' gleaming facades. He did this as part of a ten-year campaign over his claim that the bank's unauthorised transfer of funds from his account had forced him to sell his prize herd of Ayrshire cattle, ruining his livestock business. In September 2000, he was arrested while returning home for fresh supplies after making a ten-ton deposit, having already deposited two wagon-loads there in June.

A magistrates' court at Bedlington, Northumberland, gave him a concurrent 60-day gaol term, suspended for a year, for breaching a previous conditional discharge for an attack on the bank the previous year. He was also fined £100 and ordered to pay £845 compensation to the bank for clean-up costs, plus £250 in court fees. However, he did come out ahead – NatWest agreed to pay more than £300,000 in an out-of-court settlement. Cannon paid his fine and walked free from the court.

CHAPTER EIGHTEEN

Wacky Witch Laws

 T IS ALL TOO EASY TO dismiss witches as cranky old women with cats, but there was a time when the law took witchcraft seriously.

Early legislation

The Church in England was traditionally lenient on witches. In his *Liber Poenitentialis*, Theodore, Archbishop of Canterbury (668–690), laid down punishment for witchcraft as a period of fasting. And the *Confessional* of Ecgberht, Archbishop of York (735–766), set the punishment for murder by incantation at seven years fasting.

The civil authorities got in on the act with Aethelred, King of Wessex and Kent (865–871), who decided to exile witches along with whores. Then King Athelstan (925–939) instigated a get-tough policy which introduced the death penalty for murder by witchcraft, bringing it into line with murder by any other means. William the Conqueror (1066–87) reduced the sentence to banishment, although one could opt for trial by ordeal. Agnes, wife of Odo – the earliest known person accused of sorcery in England – was freed after grasping a red-hot iron.

Until around 1300, offenders were tried in ecclesiastical courts, then handed over to the secular authorities for punishment. But in the fourteenth and fifteenth centuries the civil courts took up witchcraft cases too, although the punishment was light and few suffered death. In 1371, for example, a man arrested for possessing a skull, the head of a corpse and a grimoire – a manual of magic spells and invocations – was released after promising never to perform magical rites again, although his paraphernalia were publicly burned.

In 1390, John Berking was arrested in London for soothsaying, convicted and sentenced to one hour in the pillory, two weeks' imprisonment and banishment from the City. And as late as 1467, when thousands of witches were being burned in France, one William Byng, convicted in England for gazing into a crystal ball to locate thieves, was sentenced to appear in public with a scroll on his head, carrying the words: *'Ecce sortilegus'* – 'Behold the fortuneteller.'

The crackdown

The first all-encompassing law against witchcraft was the Statute of 1542 which made it illegal to use 'invocations and conjurations' to find money or treasure that 'might be found or had in the earth or other secret places'. It was also against the law to use 'witchcrafts, enchantments and sorceries to the destruction of their neighbour's person or goods' or 'to waste, consume any person in his body, members or goods'. You were not allowed to make 'images or pictures of men, women, children, angels or devils, beasts or fowls ... to provoke any person into unlawful love or for any other unlawful intent'. And you were not allowed to 'dig up or pull down any cross or crosses'.

But it was soothsaying and fortune-telling that were considered the most serious crimes. Anyone predicting the future might foretell the death of the monarch, which could have devastating political ramifications and was tantamount to treason.

Those charged with witchcraft under the 1542 Act were not allowed to claim sanctuary. The penalty was to 'suffer the pains of death' without benefit of clergy and the 'loss and forfeiture of their lands, tenants, goods and chattels'. It sounded like another of Henry VIII's moneymaking schemes but, in fact, there is only one recorded conviction under this Act and the offender was pardoned.

Six years later, in 1547, Henry's son Edward VI repealed the Act – calling it 'very straight, sore, extreme and terrible' – along with those anti-Protestant acts Henry had passed before his break with the Catholic Church. However, the laws

against sorcery were retained when they involved murder or high treason.

Elizabethan Acts

When Elizabeth I came to the throne in 1558, the law was still relatively soft on witchcraft. In 1560, eight men – including two in holy orders – confessed to conjuration and sorcery, only to be released after a brief appearance in the pillory. They also had to swear an oath saying that they would give up such practices in future. But in 1562, the Queen nearly died of smallpox and as she had no heir, the country was afraid that it was going to be thrown back into the religious and political turmoil it had suffered under Mary Tudor.

That year, the Countess of Lennox and four others were condemned to death for treason because they 'had consulted with some pretended and cheating wizards to know how long the Queen should live', and soon after Sir Anthony Fortescue was arrested for making a horoscope of the Queen's life. Protestant England was quite willing to believe that the Roman Catholic supporters of Mary Queen of Scots were resorting to sorcery to oust Queen Elizabeth and there was an attempt to revive Henry VIII's statute. This failed, so a new Witchcraft Act was passed by both Houses of Parliament in 1562. It was supported by doctors who were eager to rid themselves of competition from 'wise women'.

Again it outlawed sorcery for the purposes of murder, bodily harm, damage to property, the recovery of treasure and obtaining unlawful love. Both the 1542 Act and the 1562 Act included a catch-all provision condemning to death all those who practised 'invocations or conjurations of evil spirits'. The new Act set the penalty for a first offence at one year's imprisonment, along with a public confession and four appearances in the pillory. A second offence attracted life imprisonment and forfeiture of property – though the widow of an executed sorcerer retained her dowry and his heirs kept their titles.

But the new Act failed to put an end to prognostications of Elizabeth's death and in 1581 a further statute was introduced, specifically outlawing horoscopes. It said: 'If any person … shall by setting or erecting any figure or by casting of nativities or by calculation or by any prophesying, witchcraft, conjuration … seek to know … how long her Majesty shall live … that then every such offence shall be a felony.'

While the penalties specified in Elizabeth's Acts were mild compared to those in Henry's, her reign saw at least 82 executions for witchcraft.

Witch trials

The first famous English witch trial took place in Chelmsford in 1566 just four years after Elizabeth's first Witchcraft Act was passed, when 63-year-old widow Agnes Waterhouse was charged with bewitching William Fynee 'who languished until 1 November [1565]'. She was familiar with a white cat called Sathan, which she turned into a toad because she wanted its fur.

One of the most eloquent witnesses against her was a 12-year-old child named Agnes Brown, who had seen a black dog with 'a face like an ape … and a pair of horns on his head' which was thought to be the white cat in disguise. The child said that the dog had tried to kill her.

'He came to me with a knife in his mouth and asked me if I was not dead,' said the child, failing to explain how the dog could talk with a knife in its mouth. 'And then he said if I would not die, then he would thrust his knife into my heart.'

The knife, she said, was a dagger although Mrs Waterhouse disputed this, saying the only knife she had in her house was a large kitchen knife. But she did admit to the attempted murder of a neighbour, numerous petty acts of vindictiveness to livestock and letting the cat suck her blood. She was also charge with 'falling out with another of her neighbours and his wife, she willed Sathan to kill him with a bloody flux, whereof he died'. However, the widow did not give testimony.

Mrs Waterhouse was cross-examined on 26 and 27 July, found guilty and hanged on 29 July 1566 – probably the first woman hanged for witchcraft in England. On the scaffold, it was said, the old woman 'yielded up her soul, trusting to be in joy with Christ her Saviour which dearly had bought her with his most precious blood'.

The second defendant was Agnes Waterhouse's 18-year-old daughter Joan, charged with bewitching her mother's accuser, 12-year-old Agnes Brown, 'who on 21 July following became decrepit in her right leg and in her right arm'. Joan threw herself on the mercy of the court and was found not guilty.

The third defendant was Elizabeth Francis, a neighbour of the Waterhouses in the village of Hatfield Peverell, Essex who had been the previous owner of the cat, Sathan. It was said that Elizabeth had learned witchcraft at the age of 12 from her grandmother, Mother Eve. She asked the cat Sathan to make her rich and he brought her 18 sheep. Then she wanted to marry a rich man named Andrew Byles. The cat said she could, but 'she must first consent that this Andrew should abuse her, and so she did. And after, when this Andrew had abused her, he would not marry her.' So the cat touched his body and he died.

But Elizabeth was now with child and 'willed Sathan to destroy it. And he bade her take a certain herb and drink it, which she did, and destroyed the child forthwith.' By this time she was having to bribe the cat with drops of blood which she obtained by pricking herself.

Elizabeth still needed a husband though, and the cat promised her the yeoman Christopher Francis 'whom she now hath, but said he was not so rich as the other, willing her to consent unto that Francis in fornication, which she did. And thereof conceived a daughter that was born with a quarter of a year after they were married'. Even then she was not happy. So the cat got rid of the child and made her husband lame.

She was also charged with bewitching the infant child of William Auger, 'who became decrepit'. She asked for her previous villainies to be taken into consideration and was gaoled for a year. Later she was charged with bewitching Mary Cocke 'who languished for ten days following'. She pleaded innocent, but was found guilty and got off with a year in gaol and four appearances in the pillory.

Then in 1579, Elizabeth appeared in court again, charged with bewitching Alice Poole, 'who languished until 1 November [1578] when she died'. Again she pleaded not guilty but was convicted and hanged, along with Ellen Smith who had been accused by a four-year-old child.

Famous witch trials also took place at Warboys in Huntingdon under the 1562 Act. But Chelmsford remained a centre of witchcraft trials up until 1645 when the Witch-Finder General, Matthew Hopkins, tried 32 women there, hanging 19 of them, by which time witchcraft laws had become even more draconian.

The Witchcraft Act of 1604

When Elizabeth I died in 1603, James VI of Scotland took the throne, becoming James I of England. His mother Mary, Queen of Scots had introduced a statute banning witchcraft, which also prohibited fortune-telling and beneficial sorcery. It also said that those seeking the help of a witch were deemed as culpable as the witches themselves and the new law started a steady stream of witch trials.

When James took the throne in Scotland, he took a hand, personally interrogating and torturing a woman named Agnes Sampson until she admitted raising storms by baptising a cat and throwing it into the sea with the severed limbs of a dead man tied to each of its paws. She said she had also made magic powder from a winding sheet and the joints of a corpse. With others of her ilk, she had made a wax dummy of the King and melted it, collected the venom from a toad after hanging it up for three days and tried to get hold of some of James's underwear so that she could smear the venom on it to make him feel 'as if he had been lying upon sharp thorns and ends of needles'. Her torment only ended when she was strangled and burned as a witch.

Another woman named in the case, Barbara Napier, was indicted for 'many treasonable conspiracies undertaken by witchcraft to have destroyed the King's person by a picture of wax … and for drowning a boat between Leigh and King-horne, wherein sixty persons were lost'. But the jury at the Edinburgh assizes dismissed the case. James was furious and charged the jury with 'wilful error on assize, acquitting a witch'. He intervened, saying, 'for an example in time coming, to make men to be more wary how they give false verdicts', and insisted that Barbara be strangled and burned at the stake, her property forfeited to him. Intimidated, the jury agreed to 'yield themselves to the King's will' and Barbara Napier was duly sentenced, but pleaded pregnancy. Later, 'nobody insisting in the pursuit of her, she was set at liberty'.

Arriving in England, James found that the English had gone soft on witchcraft, so in 1604 he passed a new Witchcraft Act, banning the resurrection of corpses for 'witchcraft, sorcery, charme or enchantment'. Murder or causing bodily harm by

sorcery was to be punished by hanging and the Act introduced a new felony – 'making a pact with the Devil or to exercise any invocation or conjuration of any evil and wicked spirit, or to consult, covenant with, entertain, employ, feed, or reward any evil and wicked spirit to or for any intent or purpose'.

This was the law that Matthew Hopkins, Witch-Finder General, used in his short-lived reign of terror in East Anglia lasting from March 1644 to July 1646.

The last execution for witchcraft took place in Scotland in 1722 and the laws against witchcraft in England and Scotland were repealed in 1736 under George II, although by an oversight, the 1562 Act remained in force in Ireland until 1821.

Pretending to be a witch

The Witchcraft Act of 1736 abolished the laws against witchcraft. Instead it sought to punish any person who shall 'pretend to exercise or use any kind of witchcraft, sorcery, enchantment or conjuration, or undertake to tell fortunes, or pretend from his or her skill or knowledge in any occult or crafty science to discover where or in what manner any goods or chattels, supposed to be stolen or lost, may be found'. They were to suffer a year's imprisonment, with an hour in the pillory every quarter.

This is the same Act that prevented any 'prosecution, suit or proceeding against … witchcraft, sorcery, enchantment or conjuration, or charging another with any such offence'. So you could practise witchcraft as long as you were doing it for real.

Paying for the privilege

While the English were content to hang their witches, the Scots burned theirs. Not only that, the victims had to pay for the privilege. When Janet Wishart and Isabel Crocker were due to be burned as witches in February 1596, the parsimonious Scots presented them with an itemised bill:

	Shillings	Pence
For twenty loads of peat to burn them	40	0
For a boll [six bushels] of coat	24	0
For four tar barrels	26	3
For fir and iron barrels	16	8
For a stake and the dressing of it	16	0
For four fathoms [24 feet] to tows [hangman's rope]	4	0
For carrying the peat, coals and barrels to the hill	8	4
To one justice for their execution	13	4

In all they were charged £11 10s. Other defendants got off with a branding on the cheek at a very reasonable 6s 8d, but all tortures had to be paid for, item by item.

On 19 November 1636, William Coke and his wife Alison Dick were burned for witchcraft at Kirkcaldy. To help them burn they were dressed in hemp garments made specially for the occasion and placed in barrels of tar. But they were too poor to pay up, so the kirk and the town council received the bill.

Margaret Dunhome – also known as Dinham or Dollmune – was executed at Burncastle in 1649. John Kincaid was paid £6 for 'brodding' her – that is, pricking her to see if she was a witch.

The executioner charged £4 14s; another £3 was paid for 'meat and drink and wine for his entertainment', plus £2 for a man with two horses to fetch him and take him home again. Two guards got £1 10s 0d a day for 30 days – £45 – and the entire bill came to £92 14s 0d in Scottish pounds, which were valued at one-sixth of an English pound. Margaret Dunhome's possessions were sold for just £27, so the outstanding bill of £65 14s 0d was presented to the owner of the estate where she had lived.

Channel Islands

Although no special laws were needed in the Channel Islands to pursue witches, Jersey passed a curious ordinance in 1591 forbidding those who have sought 'assistance from witches and diviners in their ills and afflictions … to receive any such assistance on pain of imprisonment'.

Between 1562 and 1736, there were 66 witch trials on Jersey, with at least half the accused being hanged or burned. One of the victims was Collette du Mont, who confessed to attending a sabbat in 1617. Apparently she undressed, rubbed black ointment into her back and belly and flew there. There were 15 of 16 other witches there, but she could not recognise them at first because they were blackened and disfigured. Collette then copulated with the devil, in the form of a black dog who stood on his hind legs and whose paws felt curiously like human hands.

On nearby Guernsey, an island with a population of only a few thousand, between 1558 and 1649, 20 men and 58 women were tried for witchcraft, with 50 being convicted – in England only one in five was convicted – of which three women and one man were burned alive; 24 women and four men were hanged first, then burned; three women and one man were whipped and had an ear cut off; and 21 women and five men were banished.

No law against flying

When Jane Wellman was tried before Mr Justice Powell in Gloucester in the seventeenth century on a charge of witch-craft, witnesses for the prosecution said that they had seen her fly. So the judge asked the prisoner directly: 'Prisoner, can you fly?'

'Yes, my lord,' she answered.

'Well, then, you may,' said the judge. 'There is no law against flying.'

Despite her confession, the judge instructed the jury to find her not guilty.

CHAPTER NINETEEN

Death Is No Excuse

 EATH IS NOT THE END of things – the law can pursue you beyond the grave, frequently in the most macabre manner.

Bordering on the ridiculous

Punishing a corpse was largely a Scottish practice, the first noted case being that of Roger of Mowbray, who was charged with treason against Robert the Bruce of Scotland in 1320. Although he died before his trial, he was convicted of conspiracy and his body was drawn by horses to the place of execution where he was hanged on a gallows, then beheaded.

In England, in 1400, John, Earl of Salisbury was facing trial by combat on a charge of treason, but died the day before the duel which was taken as an admission of guilt. His sureties were forfeit and a handsome fee of a hundred shillings – £5 – and 12 yards of scarlet cloth were awarded to his lawyer, Adam of Usk.

The post-mortem punishment for treason became statute law in Scotland in 1542, though the prosecution had to take place within five years of the death of the accused. During the reigns of Mary, Queen of Scots and James VI, corpses, usually embalmed for the purpose, appeared at the bar for trial. This was the continuance of a long custom carried on along the Scottish marches, where the English and Scots would carry dead bodies across the border for trial if requested. In 1597, this became a formal treaty obligation. As the Scottish Parliament succinctly put it: 'No man may excuse himself by death.' Being buried was no excuse either – traitorous corpses were disinterred to stand trial. Besides, it was thought that the best way that a man could attest that he was dead was by his attendance in court in person.

After the Restoration of the Stuart king in 1660, the corpse of Oliver Cromwell was exhumed from its resting place in Westminster Abbey and taken to Tyburn, where it was hung up besides those of the other regicides. His body was then buried beneath the gallows and his head was stuck on a pole on the top of Westminster Hall, where it remained until the end of the reign of Charles II.

Posthumous arrest

When the playwright Sheridan died, he was laid out in a friend's house in Great George Street, Westminster, where friends gathered. A man dressed in deep mourning called, saying that he had known the deceased for a long time and had come a long way in the hope of seeing his old friend one last time. With some reluctance the undertaker was persuaded to open the lid of the coffin. The man then produced a writ and a bailiff's staff, touched the corpse on the face and said, 'I arrest the corpse in the King's name for a debt of £500.'

By this time, the funeral party had arrived and, reluctant to delay the proceedings, George Canning and Lord Sidmouth wrote cheques for £250 each.

Suicide

Anyone contemplating suicide in England before 1961 was sure of success. Suicide was a capital offence so, if their attempt failed, they would be subject to criminal prosecution and sentenced to death. Similarly, if two people entered into a suicide pact and one survived, the survivor was guilty of murder. Again the penalty was death.

Until 1823, even a successful suicide was penalised. In order not to cheat the death penalty, a stake would be driven through the corpse before it was buried in unconsecrated ground, usually at a crossroads outside a town. After 1823, although a Christian burial was still not allowed, the body could be buried in a churchyard, provided – until 1882 – the burial took place between the hours of 9 and 12 at night.

Are you alive or dead when you commit suicide?

Until 1870, the crime of suicide, like treason, brought with it an attainder – the person was declared an outlaw, his blood was corrupted – meaning he could not pass on any titles to his heir

– and his property was forfeit to the Crown. This brought about a mind-boggling case in the reign of Elizabeth I, where a court had to decide whether a *felo de se* – the felony of suicide – had been committed before or after the perpetrator/victim was dead.

It is a curious principle of English law that two things cannot happen simultaneously. Time, the law holds, is infinitely divisible, so one thing must happen before the other, even if it is impossible to say which happened first. This principle has been compared to the metaphysical problem of how many angels can dance on the point of a needle – if they take up no room, there is always space for one more.

Ironically this case involved the death of a judge. In 1562, Sir James Hales, a justice of the Court of Common Pleas, died. A coroner's jury found that he had deliberately gone down to a river 'and himself therein feloniously and voluntarily drowned'. Consequently, his goods and chattels were forfeit to the Crown. However, Justice Hales had had a joint lease with his wife – was that forfeit to the Crown or did it survive with the widow?

The case came down to whether Justice Hales was alive or dead when he committed suicide. If he was alive when he committed suicide, it was decided, the lease belonged to him and was forfeit, but if he was dead when he died, it would then belong to the wife, who would retain it.

Two senior barristers argued the case for Lady Hales, whose title was presumably also vulnerable in this action. They argued that 'the death precedes the forfeiture, for until the death is fully consummated he is not *felo de se*; for if he had killed another, he should not have been a felon until the other had been dead. And for the same reason he cannot be a *felo de se* until the death of himself be fully had and consummated.'

Although, logically, both the crime, thus the forfeiture, and the death came at the same time, in law there must be a priority – 'that is, the end of life makes the commencement of the forfeiture,' the defence continued. Admittedly 'the forfeiture is so near to the death there is no meantime between them ... in consideration of law, the one precedes the other, but by no means has the forfeiture relation in any time in his life'. In other words, as the forfeiture depended on Justice Hales's death, it could not have happened within his lifetime, so it had to happen afterwards.

Four senior barristers argued the case on behalf of the Crown, one of them spelling out the Crown's reasoning this way:

> The act consists of three parts. The first is in the imagination, which is a reflection or meditation of the mind, whether or not it is convenient for him to destroy himself, and what way it can be done. The second is the resolution, which is a determination of the mind to destroy himself, and to do it in this or that particular way. The third is the perfection, which is the execution of what the mind has resolved to do. And this perfection consists of two parts, viz., the beginning and the end, and the end is the death, which is only a sequel to the act.

An account of the trial states: 'and much more to the same purport'.

The judge, Lord Dyer, pointed out that there were not four but five things to be considered in this case: 'First, the quality of the offence; secondly, to whom the offence is committed; thirdly, what shall be forfeit; fourthly, from what time the forfeiture shall commence; and fifthly, if the term here shall be taken from the wife.'

Answering these points, Sir Anthony Brown, appearing for the Crown, said, 'Sir James Hales was dead, and how did he come to his death? It may be answered, by drowning. And who drowned him? Sir James Hales. And when did he drown him? In his lifetime. So that Sir James Hales, being alive, caused Sir James Hales to die, and the act of the living man was the death of the dead man.'

The court decided for the Crown on the grounds that 'the act of the living man was the effective cause of the felony, although the latter was only consummate up to death'. And Mrs Hales found herself out on the streets.

Sad though this was, it was correct under a thirteenth-century law which maintained that the legal possession of real estate remains with a man after he dies and until his body is brought forth for burial.

The law of deodand

A deodand was originally something given up to God, but under English law it was the thing that was seen as the immediate cause of death. This, or later its monetary equivalent, was seized by the coroner's jury and given to the Crown which was supposed to put it to some pious use, such as distributed as alms.

However, a problem arose in 1840 when a steam train jumped the rails and killed four people. Four separate inquests were held, each of the juries deciding that the locomotive was the cause of death. It was assessed to be worth £125 – which seems very reasonable even for Victorian times – and each of the courts demanded a forfeit of £125.

The railway company argued that only one train had been involved in the disaster, so only one train was forfeit. It had been valued at £125, so the company was liable for no more than that.

The Court of the Exchequer then intervened with a neat solution, adjudging that a more proper valuation of the locomotive was £500, so the company should forfeit £125 to each court in each case. The law of deodand was repealed in 1846.

CHAPTER TWENTY

Rank and Rancour

N ENGLAND, EVERYONE has their place, whether they know it or not. And if they get above their station, the strange laws of old England are there to put them back down again.

Pecking order

The pecking order does not just apply to dukes and earls, but also much lower down the social scale in infinitely fine grada-tions. This was demonstrated by the case of *Ashton* v. *Jennings* which appeared before the King's Bench on 10 May 1674. It arose from a funeral which Mrs Margaret Ashton, wife of Roger Ashton, a doctor of divinity of Cambridge University and the vicar of St Andrew's, Plymouth, was invited to attend, and where she met Mrs Jennings.

As the wife of a justice of the peace, Mrs Jennings insisted that she took precedence over a vicar's wife. But Mrs Ashton refused to give way, so Mrs Jennings took it upon herself to push Mrs Ashton out of the way – as a result of which Dr Ashton took action against Mr Jennings for battery.

The defence argued Mrs Jennings had used '*molliter manus imposuit*', which means 'he laid his hands on gently' and is the legal justification for doing a wrong in order to prevent a greater wrong. She claimed she was right in doing so as the wife of a justice of the peace had precedence over the wife of a doctor of divinity. Mrs Ashton argued that, although a justice of the peace is technically an esquire, a doctor of divinity actually takes precedence. However, the precedence only comes about because the holder of a doctorate has a degree and the society status conferred by a degree is personal. It applies only to the graduate themselves and is not communicated by marriage to his wife, so Mrs Jennings was right. The wife of an esquire did take precedence.

The court admitted that it was out of its depth. The judge argued that, by entering a plea of *molliter manus imposuit*, the defendant had admitted the manhandling. Consequently Mrs Jennings was found guilty of battery. The order of precedence, the judge said, was a matter for the Court of Chivalry.

Order of precedence

Despite the ruling in the Jennings case, the Court of Chivalry does not rule on precedence, though it seems to have sat on a case in 1622. The order of precedence comes from an Anglo-Saxon document called 'Of People's Rank and the Law' drawn up between around 1029 and 1060. This was altered by the Norman Conquest and a number of charters giving rank to incoming Norman knights, noblemen and clergymen, and was altered again by the Act of Supremacy in 1534, which made Henry VIII head of the Church of England.

The House of Lords also passed a Precedence Act in 1539 which ranks peers by the 'ancienty' of their title. Special Acts of precedence have been passed when a queen marries, elevating the status of her husband and it is possible to petition the sovereign for a warrant to alter your precedence – say, if you are the brother or sister of a peer who has succeeded his grandfather or uncle, or the widow of a life peer designate, a knight bachelor designate or the heir apparent of a baronet.

However, the modern order of precedence is largely governed by a Lord Chamberlain's order of 1520, as amended in 1595 specifying such vital things as: 'Earls' younger sons be born as barons [and] that they shall go beneath all barons' and viscounts' eldest sons and above all baronets and their wives to go beneath all baronesses and viscounts' daughters and above all baronets' wives.'

As a result we now have an order of precedence which starts with the Queen, who for this purpose is classified as a man. After the Duke of Edinburgh, the Prince of Wales, the Queen's younger sons, the dukes of the blood royal and Prince Michael of Kent, we get the 'Viceregent in Spirituals' – an office vacant since 1540. Further on we get the Lord High Constable, who has not been seen (except at coronations) since 1521, the Lord High Treasurer, who has not been commissioned since 1714 and the Lord High Admiral, who has been missing since 1828.

Comfortingly, right up there with the Prime Minister and the Archbishop of Canterbury are the Lord Great Chamberlain and the Master of the Horse, who are still around. Following them is the Lord Privy Seal.

Further down the ranking you will be glad to know that younger sons of the dukes of the royal blood still outrank the eldest sons of marquises, and that wives of Companions of the Distinguished Service Order outrank the wives of Members of the Royal Victorian Order (Fourth Class), while wives of Members of the Royal Victorian Order (Fifth Class) in turn outrank wives of Members of the Order of the British Empire – not to mention wives of the younger sons of baronets and knights.

More swearing

Swearing once cost you more if you were from the aristocracy (see The Laws that Never Were, page 56). Under the Profane Oaths Act of 1745 the penalty for cursing or swearing was one shilling for an 'everyday labourer, common soldier, common sailor and common seaman'; two shillings for 'every other person, under the degree of gentleman'; and five shillings for every person 'of or above the degree of gentleman'.

The penalty was doubled for a second conviction and trebled for a third and subsequent convictions. However, the courts were presented with a problem in 1863, when a 'mealman' called Scott 'unlawfully did profanely curse one profane curse … twenty times repeatedly'. Scott fell into the two shillings category, but did his tirade count as a single offence or twenty? The justices took the latter view, multiplied two shillings by 20 and fined the accused £2. The legal commentator R.E. Megarry pointed out that this proves 'mere repetition is no economy, and variety no extravagance'. The law was repealed in 1967.

Privileges

There are certain privileges you expect from being upper class. In 1734, the Scottish Lord Mordington sought his release after being arrested because he was a peer of the realm. He got the bailiff to swear an affidavit saying that 'when he arrested the said Lord, he was so mean in his apparel, as having a worn-out suit of cloaths, and a dirty shirt on, and but sixpence in his pocket, he could not suppose him to be a peer of Great Britain; and therefore through inadvertancy arrested him'. The court discharged the lord and made the bailiff ask the peer to pardon him.

Disciplining your servants

It is always a problem to know how to discipline servants, so in 1697, a court gave a decision on the matter. 'If a master gives correction to his servant,' the ruling read, 'it ought to be with a proper instrument, as a cudgel, &c. And then if by accident a blow gives death, this would be manslaughter – the same law of a school-master. But the sword is not a proper instrument for correction, and the cruelty of the cut will make a malice implied.' The result: murder.

Upper class on trial

Under English law it is your right to be tried by your peers. This is guaranteed by Clause 39 of Magna Carta, signed at Runnymede in 1215, or Clause 29 of the 1297 version quoted above. That meant, until the passing of the 1948 Criminal Justice Act, Clause 30, that members of the House of Lords had the right to be tried by the House, if it was sitting. If Parliament was in recess, the hearing would take place in the Court of the High Steward, with only the Law Lords present.

Even in 1935, this only applied in cases of treason or a felony, other crimes being tried before ordinary courts. In December that year, Edward Southwell Russell, 26th Baron de Clifford, insisted on his right to be tried before the House of Lords for the manslaughter of Douglas George Hopkins, who had been killed in a car accident on the Kingston by-pass in August. This was the last trial to take place before the Lords Spiritual and Temporal, Peers of the Realm, the Archbishops and Bishops, and the Judges.

The peers were marshalled in the Palace of Westminster's Royal Gallery by the Norroy Kings of Arms, Chief Herald north of the Trent, while the defendant was in the custody of the Gentleman Usher of Black Rod. Presiding was the Lord Chancellor, the Lord High Steward, who sat before the throne. The Norroy and Black Rod approached the Lord High Steward, bowing low three times on the way, and presented him with his symbol of office, the White Staff. The trial then got under way.

After hearing the prosecution and the defence, the peers and judges filed out, and the Lord High Steward asked each of them in turn, starting with the most junior, whether they found the defendant 'guilty or not guilty'. Each had to reply either 'guilty upon my honour' or 'not guilty upon my honour'. As it was, they unanimously found de Clifford not guilty.

Bigamy

Before peers lost the right to be tried before the House of Lords, a woman could be married to two men and not be found guilty of bigamy – if the first marriage was to a commoner and the second to a peer of the realm. As a peeress, she would have had the right to be tried by the House of Lords, who would have been obliged to acquit her – if they had tried to convict her, they would have established the first marriage in law, which would mean that she was not a peeress and they would have no jurisdiction. Equally, if a crown court tried to convict, it would acknowledge the rank conferred by her second marriage, negating its own jurisdiction.

CHAPTER TWENTY-ONE

Long Arm of the Law

T IS ONE THING TO WRITE a strange law down on paper, quite another thing to enforce it. Consequently more strange laws were passed trying to put the law into practice.

Declining a knighthood

In 1233, Roger of Dudley was summoned to court to be knighted but realising that the honour brought with it a great deal of expense, he refused to appear. Overnight it became against the law to decline a knighthood and a writ was issued, which read: 'Because Roger de Someri, at the feast of Pentecost last past, had not appeared before the King to be girded with the military girdle, the Sheriff of Worcestershire is hereby commanded to seize the house of Dudley and all other lands of the said Roger within his jurisdiction, for the King's use; and to keep them with all the cattle found upon them, so that nothing may be moved off without the King's permission.'

Outlaws

Until quite recently, if you were rich enough or noble enough, you could openly flout the law. In the late sixteenth century, the then William de Birmingham went out with a hundred men to rob travellers and there was nothing the authorities could do about it.

In 1592, Lord Edward Dudley had a dispute with the neighbouring Lyttelton family, raised an army of 150 men and, one night, stole all the cattle from the Lytteltons' estate. The Lytteltons went to court and got a judgement against Dudley, who was ordered to return the cattle. He refused and posted guards with orders to cut the bailiffs to pieces, so the Lytteltons took the matter into their own hands and repossessed the cattle by force with 60 men. Dudley then raised 700 men, who fetched back the cattle again and killed them, for which Dudley and 80 of his followers were indicted. The proceedings dragged on for four years until a settlement was finally made.

Meanwhile, Lord Dudley's son Ferdinando bought a property worth £1,200 from a widow named Martha Grosvenor, but he only paid a £100 deposit and refused to give her the balance. She sued in the Court of the Exchequer for the rest of the money and obtained judgement, which Ferdinando ignored. The following year, she got a second decree in her favour, so when Ferdinando again took no notice, the court pursued him for costs. He agreed to pay these and the money he owed the widow, but failed to do so, so an order evicting him from the property was issued. He failed to comply for nine years and it was twelve years after he had first moved in before he settled with the widow.

Hue and cry

In 1577 a servant had been robbed on Gadds Hill, which lay within the hundred of Gravesend. His master tried to sue Gravesend under the Statute of Winchester of 1285, which says that 'cries shall be solemnly made in all counties, hundreds, markets, fairs and other places where great resort of people is', so that robbers and felons might be caught.

But the men of Gravesend would have none of it. They said that since 'time out of mind, felons had used to rob at Gadds Hill' – in other words, it was always happening, so why kick up a fuss? The court found against them, reasoning that otherwise they would be creating no-go areas where people were free to steal. And, under a statute of Elizabeth I, the hundred had to compensate the victim with half the amount he had lost. This was a forerunner of the Riot (Damages) Act of 1886, still in force, which says that people whose property is damaged, destroyed or stolen during a riot should be compensated out of the 'police rate'.

However, while the court was sympathetic to the victim, later more religious legislators were not. In the Sunday Observance Act of 1677, Parliament said that the hundred was not responsible for the safety of people travelling on a Sunday – if the people were so irreligious as to travel on the Lord's Day, they deserved anything that befell them.

Thief-takers

In the 1720s, there was no organised police force and magistrates would pay rewards to encourage people to catch and turn in criminals, so a number of professional 'thief-takers' grew up, one of them a man named Jonathan Wild. He was so successful that rich people and even the government turned to him for help. His record was impressive – he recovered thousands of stolen items and sent 67 people to the gallows, earn-

ing himself a small fortune in rewards in the process. The secret of his success was that he ran an underworld gang who did most of the stealing, so it was easy to get the stolen items back, while anyone who got in his way was named as the thief and hanged. Eventually, he was caught selling stolen goods, his scheme was unmasked and he went to the gallows himself.

Police

In 1748, the writer Henry Fielding was appointed as magistrate at the court in Bow Street where he found that the constables who patrolled the City were so incompetent that he sacked them and hired six men of his own. These became the Bow Street Runners. Their success in capturing highwaymen encouraged the government to give him the money to increase his squad to ten. When Fielding died in 1754, his brother John took over. Although he was equally successful in stamping out the gangs of highway robbers who preyed on travellers on the turnpikes around the City, the government withdrew their funding and soon crime had returned to its former levels. The situation became so dire that the patrols resumed in 1805, and in 1829 Home Secretary Sir Robert Peel expanded the police force to cover the whole of the metropolitan area – from Camberwell in the south to Highgate in the north – his men becoming known as Peelers, or Bobbies, after their founder.

Breaking and entering

The power of a bailiff is restricted by law – he cannot, for example, break the outer door of a debtor's house to gain entry to arrest the debtor, but he can use any trick, stratagem or false-hood to get inside peaceably. Once in, he can break through inner doors if necessary, and if he has been inside but has been ejected he can break back into the house.

He can also break into a third party's house if he has reason to believe that the debtor is seeking refuge there – though he must ask if he can enter peaceably and give his reason for seek-ing entry first. But if he breaks in and the debtor is not there the bailiff can be prosecuted for trespass.

CHAPTER TWENTY-TWO

The Peculiarities of Prerogative

OT ALL LAW IN ENGLAND BELONGS to Parliament and the courts, for there is also the royal prerogative. Much of this has been usurped by the government, which can – using prerogative powers – go to war without the approval of Parliament. However, not all prerogative power has been taken away, some still resting with the monarch. And there are plenty of strange laws surrounding the Crown itself.

Whales and sturgeons

Under a statute called *Prerogativa Regis* – 'Of the King's Prerogative' – or the Wreck of the Sea Act, which was signed into law in 1324 by Edward II, 'the King shall have throughout the realm, whales and great sturgeons taken in the sea or elsewhere within the realm'.

In medieval times, any whale caught off the coast of England was cut in two. By custom, the head went to the King, while the tail was sent to the Queen to provide whalebone for her stays. However, in 1970 the Queen was persuaded to give up her right to captured whales and the Law Commission sent a recommendation to Parliament that this prerogative be abolished. However, in 1971, the repeal of the 1324 law was voted down by the House of Lords, so whales still belong to the monarch – though catching them is now outlawed by international treaty.

When it comes to conservation, the law still has its uses. In 2001, Norwegian whalers, who had been catching minke whales in the Atlantic on the flimsy pretext that they were conducting a population survey, were banned from carrying out similar 'research' in British waters.

Royal pets

The Queen's corgis will be grateful to know that they are safe from being molested by lesser breeds. An Act passed by George I promises that the 'severest Penaltys will be suffered by any

commoner who doth permit his animal to have carnal knowledge of a pet of the Royal House'.

Royal Marriages Act

The early Hanoverians were fairly badly behaved and when George III came to the throne he tried to clean up the family's act by signing into law the Royal Marriages Act of 1772, through which he aimed to ensure that his sons and daughters married people he approved of.

The Act read: 'That no descendent of the body of His late Majesty King George the Second, male or female (other than the issue of princesses who have married, or may hereafter marry, into foreign families) shall be capable of contracting matrimony without previous consent of His Majesty, His Heirs or Successors ... and that every marriage, or matrimonial contract, of any descendant, without such consent first and obtained, shall be null and void, to all intents and purposes whatsoever.'

However, this did not prevent his children marrying people he did not approve of. It meant that the King's offspring could marry whoever they liked and if the marriage had not received the consent of the King, they could get a quick divorce. It was, as one MP put it when it was going through the House, 'an Act for ... the Encouragement of Adultery and Fornication'.

As such it worked very well indeed. After bedding an impressive succession of mistresses, George's heir, who became the Prince Regent and later George IV, met Mrs Maria Fitzherbert, twice divorced and a Catholic. Still only 23, George failed to consult his father about the marriage – which would have been illegal anyway under the Act of Settlement of 1701 which prevented the heir to the throne marrying a Catholic. So he paid £500 to get an Anglican priest out of debtors' prison, who, on the promise of a bishopric, performed a marriage ceremony.

Mrs Fitzherbert bore the Prince of Wales ten children, but he had no problem divorcing her when it was convenient. To pay off his enormous debts, he agreed to a disastrous marriage to Caroline of Brunswick, then sought comfort with a fresh series of mistresses; but Caroline would not be dismissed so lightly even though he tried to divorce her twice. The case had to be heard by the House of Lords and, although every detail of Caroline's strenuous love life was related to a packed House, it was decided that what was sauce for the gander was sauce for the goose.

George IV's younger brother, who became William IV, was as debauched as his older brother and spent much of his youth frequenting whorehouses. He caused a scandal when he returned from Jamaica with a West Indian concubine called 'Wowski', before setting up home with an actress called Mrs Jordan, though her real name was Dorothea Bland. They, too, had ten children but when, after 20 years, she lost her charms, William abandoned her and married Princess Adelaide of Saxe-Coburg and Meiningen, while Dorothea died penniless and alone in France.

Prince Edward abandoned his mistress of 25 years standing to marry, briefly, Princess Victoria of Leinigen – which led to the birth of the future Queen Victoria.

Princess Augusta fell in love with an equerry and, never daring to ask for her father's permission, they married in secret.

Princess Amelia also seems to have had a secret marriage to an equerry, while Princess Elizabeth fell pregnant at the age of 16, then waited until she was 47 before marrying the dull Prince of Hesse-Homberg.

Meanwhile Prince Augustus Frederick married openly in Rome in direct contravention of the Royal Marriages Act. When the marriage was declared invalid by an ecclesiastical court in England Augustus Frederick abandoned his wife and children for an income of £12,000 and the Duchy of Sussex. He eventually sued for custody of the children and to deprive his ex of the title of duchess, then married the widow of a City grocer.

George III's youngest son, Adolphus, Duke of Cambridge, avoided problems by living in Germany with Augusta of Hesse-Cassel – so George III's attempt to bring a little respectability to the family with the Royal Marriages Act can only be judged a resounding failure.

The Act is still in force, though in 1936 a special bill had to be rushed through Parliament waiving both the Act of Settlement and the Royal Marriages Act in the case of Edward VIII so that he could marry the divorcee Mrs Wallis Simpson.

Similar provision might have to be made for Prince Charles if ever he wants to marry Camilla Parker-Bowles. Under the Royal Marriages Act the monarch's ban only lasts up to the age of 25, but after that, an heir still needs the monarch's permission and has to wait a year if it is refused. Even then, the Act gives Parliament the absolute right to veto any marriage. What's more, Camilla's former husband, Andrew Parker-Bowles, is a Catholic, which could make her ineligible under the Act of Settlement.

The traitorous queen of hearts

Under the Treason Act of 1351, anyone who 'do violate the king's companion, or the king's eldest daughter unmarried, or the wife of the king's eldest son' is committing treason. Until 1998, the penalty was death.

Strangely, when Diana made her famous television appearance asking to be our queen of hearts, she was also admitting treason. The penalty, under the 1351 Act, was to be burned at the stake. What was she planning to wear for the occasion?

High treason to burn a brothel

In 1663, a gang of apprentice boys stood trial for high treason for trying to demolish a 'disorderly house'. Hearing the case at the Old Bailey Chief Justice Sir John Kelynge told the jury: 'The prisoners are indicted for levying war against the King. By "levying war" is not only meant when a body is gathered together as an army, but if a company of people will go about any public reformation, this is high treason. These people do pretend their design was against brothels; now for men to go about to pull down brothels, with a captain and an ensign, and weapons – if this thing is to be endured, who is safe?' They were convicted and punished accordingly.

Again, during the reign of Queen Anne, High Church rioters who demolished a brothel were charged with treason. At their trial, Chief Justice Sir Thomas Parker explained: 'A brothel is a nuisance and may be punished as such, and being a particular nuisance to anyone, if he enters to abate it may only be guilty of a riot; but if he will presume to pull down all brothels, he has taken the Queen's right out of her hand, and has committed high treason, by compassing her death, and levying war against her in her realm.'

Once more the defendants were found guilty and Justice Parker sentenced them to be hanged, drawn and quartered. Later, they were reprieved and pardoned.

These two cases caused the distinguished legal writer Lord John Campbell to contemplate the special place occupied by the brothel in the affections of judges. Relating the 1663 Kelynge case in his nineteenth-century four-volume *The Chief Justices of England*, he added as a footnote his recollection of an incident after a famous bordello burned down one night in London with the loss of several lives. The following morning the next judicial term began and, when the judges assembled in the Chancellor's chambers, Lord Chief Baron Macdonald exclaimed: 'It gives me heartfelt pleasure, my dear brethren, to see you all here quite safe.'

In the witness box

When a bill to impeach the Duke of Buckingham was passed in 1626, he proposed to call Charles I in his defence. The problem was that no one could decide whether to call the monarch was legal or not. As the sovereign is the fount of justice – all criminal prosecutions are done in the name of the Crown – the evidence he gave could not be questioned. But since the King could not be prosecuted for perjury if he lied, his testimony would be given without 'temporal sanction', making it worthless under English law.

On the other hand, the defendant might be deprived of a defence if the monarch could not be called and learned opinion urged that justice had to be paramount to all technical rules. While the judicial authorities were debating the situation, Charles sent word that they would not be allowed to settle the matter as any decision might have unforeseen consequences for his crown. Instead, Charles dissolved Parliament. Buckingham's case was then tried before the Royal Court of the Star Chamber where, to no one's surprise, the charges were dismissed.

Lord John Campbell applied his not inconsiderable brain to this vexed question of whether the monarch could be called as a witness and decided that 'the sovereign, if so pleased, might be examined as a witness in any case, civil or criminal, but must be sworn, although there would be no temporal sanction to the oath'. And he pointed out that James I had given a written statement concerning what had taken place in his hearing, in a case in Chancery. However, in other cases, the monarch's written evidence has been refused – it seems that you can get as many legal opinions on this question as you have lawyers. Consequently, to this day, no one knows whether you can call the monarch in your defence in a court case.

Burying the crown

Although there is no statute that prohibits the British crown being removed from the country, it has always been regarded as a convention of the constitution that all the royal regalia has to remain on British soil. It is thought that this convention came about because when medieval kings were pursuing their frequent foreign adventures their creditors insisted they leave the crown behind as collateral to cover their war debts.

There are two state crowns: one is Edward the Confessor's crown and is the Crown of England; the other is the Imperial State Crown. Made from jewels sent from the Indian subcontinent, the latter is the Indian Crown and was used when George V was crowned King-Emperor in 1911. Not only has it not been returned to the subcontinent after independence, but it too is not allowed out of the country – it was adjudged unconstitutional for George VI to take it with him to Canada in 1939 to open the parliament in Ottawa. The Imperial State Crown has not even become the crown of the British Commonwealth, but remains part of the regalia of England and is locked up in the Tower of London.

Quaint though this convention may be, it caused real problems at the beginning of the Second World War when Britain faced the threat of invasion, for the royal regalia could not simply be spirited out of the country for safekeeping. This meant that the crown jewels were buried in a location known to only three people; and the Scottish royal regalia were given similar treatment north of the border. The 1706 Act of Union states that 'the crown, sceptre and sword of state ... continue to be kept as they are within that part of the United Kingdom now called Scotland and that they shall so remain in all time coming (notwithstanding the Union)'.

Who owns your passport?

Who owns your passport? You may think that you do as you paid £42 for it . However, on the cover, it bears the Royal Arms, indicating that it is the property of the sovereign. Then, if you look inside, you will find a note that reads: 'This passport remains the property of Her Majesty's Government in the United Kingdom and may be withdrawn at any time.'

When the matter of who owns a person's passport was raised in the House of Lords in 1955, Earl Jowitt, a former attorney-general and solicitor-general, pointed out that the government could not own anything as, in law, there was no such entity.

Replying to Earl Jowitt, the Minister of State for Foreign Affairs, the Marquess of Reading, said that the granting of passports was a royal prerogative exercised through Her Majesty's ministers, particularly the Foreign Secretary. But he could not enlighten the House as to who owned them and the matter remains unresolved.

Rockall

In September 1955, Commander Richard Connell, captain of HMS *Vidal*, which was in port in Northern Ireland, received orders from Her Majesty the Queen. They read:

> When Our ship *Vidal* is in all respects ready for sea and all necessary personnel are embarked, you are to leave Londonderry on September 14, 1955, or the earliest date thereafter. Thence you will proceed to the island of Rockall. On arrival at Rockall you will effect a landing and hoist the Union flag on whatever spot appears the most suitable or practicable, and you will then take possession of the island on Our behalf … When the landing has been effected and the flag has been hoisted you will cement a commemorative plaque to the rock.

Rockall is an isolated, uninhabited, pudding-shaped sea rock situated in the middle of the North Atlantic. Just 25 metres long, 30 metres wide and 19 metres high, about 300 miles from the coasts of Scotland, Ireland and Iceland. It had long been a disputed territory – the UK, Ireland, Iceland and even Denmark had been bickering over it for years. But in 1955 Britain decided to resolve the situation by seizing it. Although nothing much lives there apart from colonies of gannets, seagulls, lichens, limpets and periwinkles, there was always the possibility that oil and gas might be found in the surrounding seabed and, at that time, the waters around it were teeming with fish.

The *Vidal* was chosen for this imperial task as it was Rear Admiral T.E. Vidal who fixed the exact position of the rock in 1831. She duly arrived off Rockall at dusk on 17 September, but stood off as the island was a hazard during the hours of darkness. The only piece of land within hundreds of square miles of open sea, it has been responsible for at least two major shipwrecks: the *Helen of Dundee* in 1824 and the *Norge* in 1904, when over 600 people were killed.

At daylight the following morning, the ship's helicopter lowered Sergeant Brian Peel, a Royal Marine Commando and experienced climber, onto the rock. He was followed by another Royal Marine Commando, an ornithologist and Lieutenant Commander Desmond Scott, First Lieutenant of the *Vidal* and commander of the landing party. An 8-foot, prefabricated flagpole was erected and at 10.16 a.m. BST the Union Jack was raised as Lieutenant Commander Scott announced: 'In the name of Her Majesty Queen Elizabeth II, I hereby take possession of the Island of Rockall.'

The *Vidal* then fired a 21-gun salute, a plaque was cemented in place announcing the annexation and, after three hours occupation, the landing party withdrew, mission accomplished.

However, although the island had been seized by the Royal Navy, it had not become part of the United Kingdom or the British Empire and became what is known as a Royal Peculiar. It belonged to the Queen, in her public capacity, like Westminster Abbey, St George's Chapel in Windsor and three other royal chapels. It was not the responsibility of the UK government, any more than it was of the Canadian government. On Rockall, the sovereign's jurisdiction was absolute.

This situation continued for 16 years, until an Act of

Parliament in 1971 handed Rockall over to Scotland, where it became part of Invernesshire. The territorial dispute flared again after the Cod War of 1975–1976, when the UK government declared the sea within 50 miles of the rock to be territorial waters. This prompted a renewed diplomatic battle with Ireland, Iceland and Denmark over the status of Rockall as an island and to consolidate Britain's claim, Atlantic rower John Ridgeway and SAS man Tom McLean occupied the barren island for a month at separate times during the 1980s. The status of Rockall remains unresolved to the present day.

Succeeding twice

It is possible to succeed twice to the British throne by natural succession. If the King dies and is survived by a widow but no son, his eldest daughter or some other heir to the throne will succeed. But this succession is not absolute. If the dowager Queen gave birth to the dead King's posthumous son, the son would succeed, displacing his older sister or other claimant. If the son then died without having children of his own, the heir who originally assumed the Crown, if they were still alive, would do so again.

This principle was enacted by statute in the Regency Act of 1830, soon after William IV succeeded to the throne. If William and Queen Adelaide had no children, Victoria would succeed, 'subject to and saving the rights of any issue of his said majesty which may afterwards be born of her said majesty'. The oath of allegiance to Queen Victoria was qualified in the same way.

CHAPTER TWENTY-THREE

Transports of Delight

 URING THE VICTORIAN ERA politicians were fond of passing new railways Acts, while nowadays there is legislation covering every aspect of motoring. But since the time of Queen Anne the form of transportation that has attracted the most legislation is the Hackney carriage – the good old black taxi. There have been over 37 Acts regulating the taxi in that time, and many of them are still in force.

The London taxi

It is, in fact, illegal to hail a cab while it is in motion – technically you should go to a rank or 'place appointed'. No other vehicle is allowed to park in a taxi rank which is required to have a water trough so the horses could take a drink.

The cabby is supposed to ask each of his passengers if they are suffering from any 'notifiable disease such as smallpox or the plague'. As carrying suffers is illegal, he should technically carry out an on-the-spot medical examination and if the passenger were to pass away during the journey he would be committing another offence as it is illegal for a taxi driver to carry corpses or rabid dogs. The cabby is also required to carry out a thorough search of his vehicle before allowing a fare to go on its way – it is the cabby's responsibility, not the passenger's, to see that nothing is left behind.

The law requiring a cabby to carry a bale of hay on the roof of his cab to feed the horse was repealed in 1976, and they no longer have to carry a nosebag on the side of the vehicle or a sack of oats. It has long since been assumed that the law requiring the cabby to carry 'adequate foodstuffs for the horse' meant a tank full of diesel.

A cabby who drives too slowly or holds up the traffic can be prosecuted for 'loitering'; one who goes too fast can be prosecuted for 'furious driving'. And whether furious or not, it is expressly forbidden for a driver to make 'insulting gestures'.

As cabbies were not allowed to leave their cab on the public highway, the driver was allowed to urinate in public, as long as it was on the rear wheel of the vehicle with his right hand placed on it. This law was enacted when all cabbies were men – how it applies now in the age of women drivers is unclear.

Cycling

After the introduction of the safety bike in 1885, cycling became a craze in England, but it soon presented problems on the roads. Cyclists speeding past horse-drawn vehicles frightened the animals and often led to angry encounters. In the county of Middlesex in 1888, the local authority passed a ruling that cyclists should either dismount when a horse-drawn vehicle approached or, if they wanted to pass, they should 'inquire politely of the carriage driver for permission to overtake'.

Bath chairs

In the late Victorian era, a law was passed banning Bath chairs – once the favoured mode of transport of the elderly and gout ridden – being pushed three abreast in the area of St James's and Green Park.

Red flag

The Locomotives Act 1865 required that any vehicle – other than those which relied on animal power – travelling on the road should be preceded by a man on foot carrying a red flag at a distance of not less than 60 yards; any such vehicle should employ at least three people to drive it; a maximum speed of two miles an hour was allowed in town and four miles an hour in the country; and the vehicle had to stop instantly if a horse rider or the driver of a horse-drawn carriage raised their hand. The fine for any such offences was a maximum of £10. These provisions were repealed for light vehicles in 1896 and the top speed was raised to 14 miles an hour. On 28 January 1896, Walter Arnold of East Peckham, Kent, became the first man to be prosecuted for speeding when he was caught doing eight miles an hour in a built-up area by a traffic policeman who pursued him on a bike. Exceeding the urban speed limit by a massive six miles an hour, he was fined one shilling – 5p.

In 1903, the speed limit was raised to 20 miles an hour on the open road, ten in town, but not before speed traps had been introduced in England the previous year. In an effort to crack down on reckless drivers, policemen were stationed behind hedges with stopwatches and bicycles. One of the earliest offenders, caught doing a breakneck 12 miles an hour, was Lord Montagu of Beaulieu, whose collection of vintage cars now form the nucleus of the National Motor Museum.

Arresting aliens

The Outer Space Act 1986 prohibits ordinary citizens launching a 'space object' and 'carrying on other activities in space'. Under Section 9 magistrates are given the power to issue warrants and 'use reasonable force' to turn back an alien invasion provided, of course, that the aliens do not have a licence to invade. The Act defines 'outer space' to include 'the moon and other celestial bodies' and applies to 'any activity carried on in outer space'. The courts are required to maintain a 'register of space objects' in which details will have to be entered of their 'nodal period, inclination, apogee and perigee' and operators are compelled to provide details of 'basic orbital parameters'.